Preface

Child care and protection is a vast area of law, which constantly changes and develops. We cannot cover everything here, but we hope this book gives an overview and basic practical guide through the maze of the Children Act 1989 and its subordinate legislation, guidance and case law, taking into account recent changes in law, guidance and social work practice, including the Human Rights Act 1998, the European Convention for the Protection of Human Rights and Fundamental Freedoms, and the new Framework for Assessment of Children in Need and their Families, with its new developments in care planning. We also bear in mind the provisions of the UN Convention on the Rights of the Child.

Child care and protection practice is not just a matter of law. In order to generate effective action on behalf of children and their families and to represent parents and local authorities effectively, practitioners also need to understand the work and concerns of social services, police, health practitioners, and other agencies involved in child protection.

The Law Society recognised the need to broaden the expertise of members of its Children Panel (which will now cover representation of children, adults and local authorities) and has extended the qualifying course to include a wider range of relevant sociological, psychological and practice issues.

Family law advocacy, and giving evidence as a professional or expert witness, can be daunting. Confidence can be gained with careful case preparation, together with an understanding of court procedures and the mutual expectations of courts and professional witnesses, and we have included here a few insights from practice.

We intend 'he' and 'she' to include either gender, where relevant, in this book.

Child care and protection is a very rewarding area of law in which to work. It is a privilege to work with children and their families, and with all those who are involved in child care and protection.

Barbara Mitchels and Helen James
March 2001

Child Care Protection

Law & Practice

THIRD EDITION

BARBARA MITCHELS,
LLB, DIP COUNS & PSY, UKRC, MRCM
CHILDREN PANEL SOLICITOR (RTD)

WITH

HELEN JAMES, RCCYP, CQSW
GUARDIAN AD LITEM

SERIES EDITOR
CM BRAND, SOLICITOR

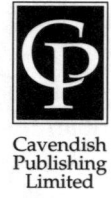

Cavendish
Publishing
Limited

London • Sydney

Third edition first published in Great Britain 2001 by Cavendish Publishing Limited, The Glass House, Wharton Street, London WC1X 9PX

Telephone: (0)20 7278 8000   Facsimile: (0)20 7278 8080
Email: info@cavendishpublishing.com
Website: www.cavendishpublishing.com

Mitchels, Barbara
Child care protection law and practice – 3rd ed – (Practice notes series)
1 Children – legal status, laws, etc – England   2 Children – legal status, laws, etc – Wales
I Title II James, Helen
344.4'2'0327

ISBN 1 85941 455 9
Printed and bound in Great Britain

Acknowledgments

With grateful thanks to Helen James, Guardian ad Litem, for her assistance with the sections of the book relating to recent developments in care planning and assessments and, also, for her wisdom, support, and sense of humour as a colleague on training and course facilitation over the years, particularly with Children Panel training.

I would like to thank all those who have given their permission to include quotations, references and materials.

Thank you, too, for the advice and help of children and families over the years who are better sources of information than any law book!

Finally, especial thanks to John, Ruth, Josie, Anne Marie,and Mark, for their tolerance, patience and fortifying cups of tea whilst this was being written!

Barbara Mitchels

Contents

1 Sources and Introduction to the Children Act 1989, Subordinate Legislation and Guidance

1.1 Statutes

- Abortion Act 1967
- Access to Health Records Act 1990
- Access to Medical Reports Act 1988
- Access to Justice Act 1999
- Adoption Act 1976
- Child Abduction Act 1984
- Child Abduction and Custody Act 1985
- Child Support Act 1991
- Children Act 1989
- Children and Young Persons Act 1933
- Children and Young Persons Act 1969
- County Courts Act 1984
- Crime and Disorder Act 1998
- Domestic Proceedings and Magistrates' Courts Act 1978
- Domicile and Matrimonial Proceedings Act 1973
- Education Act 1996
- Family Law Act 1986
- Family Law Act 1996
- Family Law Reform Act 1969

- Family Law Reform Act 1987
- Foster Children Act 1980
- Human Fertilisation and Embryology Act 1990
- Human Rights Act 1998
- Local Authority Social Services Act 1970
- Mental Health Act 1983
- Police and Criminal Evidence Act 1984
- Protection from Harassment Act 1997
- Protection of Children Act 1999
- Race Relations Act 1976
- Rehabilitation of Offenders Act 1974
- Sexual Offences Act 1956
- Supreme Court Act 1981
- Surrogacy Arrangements Act 1985

1.2   Conventions and protocols

- UN Convention on the Rights of the Child (in force in the UK on 15 January 1992)
- European Convention for the Protection of Human Rights and Fundamental Freedoms
- Protocols made under the European Convention for the Protection of Human Rights and Fundamental Freedoms

1.3   Statutory instruments

- Access to Personal Files (Social Services) Regulations 1989 SI 1989/206
- Access to Personal Files (Social Services) (Amendment) Regulations 1991 SI 1991/1587
- Adoption Rules 1984 SI 1984/265
- Arrangements for Placement of Children (General) Regulations 1991 SI 1991/890
- Blood tests (Evidence of Paternity) Regulations 1971 SI 1971/1861
- Children (Allocation of Proceedings) Order 1991 SI 1991/1677
- Children (Allocation of Proceedings, Appeals) Order 1991 SI 1991/1801

- Children (Secure Accommodation) Regulations 1991 SI 1991/1505
- Children (Secure Accommodation No 2) Regulations 1991 SI 1991/2034
- Children (Admissibility of Hearsay Evidence) Order 1993 SI 1993/621
- Civil Procedure Rules 1998 SI 1998/3132
- Community Legal Service (Financial Regulations) 2000 SI 2000/516
- Community Legal Service (Cost Protection) Regulations 2000 SI 2000/824
- Community Legal Service (Costs) Regulations 2000 SI 2000/441
- Contact with Children Regulations 1991 SI 1991/891
- County Court Rules 1981 SI 1981/1687
- Family Law Act 1996 (Part IV) (Allocation of Proceedings) Order 1997 SI 1997/1896
- Family Proceedings Courts (Children Act 1989) Rules 1991 SI 1991/1395
- Family Proceedings Rules 1991 SI 1991/1247
- Family Proceedings (Miscellaneous Amendment) Rules 1999 SI 1999/1012
- Foster Placement (Children) Regulations 1991 SI 1991/910
- Guardians ad Litem and Reporting Officers (Panels) Regulations 1991 SI 1991/201
- Guardians ad Litem and Reporting Officers (Panels) (Amendment) Regulations 1997 SI 1997/1662
- Parental Responsibility Agreement Regulations 1991 SI 1991/1478
- Parental Responsibility Agreement Regulations 1994 SI 1994 /3157
- Representations Procedure (Children) Regulations 1991 S1 1991/894
- Review of Childrens' Cases Regulations 1991 SI 1991/895
- Rules of the Supreme Court 1965 SI 1965/1776

1.4   Case law

Case law has been referred to in the text and references cited there. It remains essential to monitor case law developments in this field as new issues are examined in the courts and tested through the appeal process.

1.5   Practice directions

- *Adopted Children Register: Restriction on Disclosure* [1999] 1 FLR 315
- *Children Act 1989 – Applications by Children* [1993] 1 FLR 1008

1.6   Guidance

Current recommended interdisciplinary child protection procedures are set out in *Working Together to Safeguard Children* (1999, London: HMSO) and the *Guidance and Regulations* made under the Children Act 1989. These guidance volumes are issued under s 7 of the Local Authority Social Services Act 1970 and, therefore, should be followed by local authorities. A local authority must justify any departure from their provisions. Unjustifiable failure to comply may form the basis for complaint or judicial review. In Scotland, reference should be made to *Protecting Children* (1998, Edinburgh: Scottish Office).

- *The Children Act 1989: Guidance and Regulations* (London: HMSO) comprise:

Volume 1	Court Orders
Volume 2	Family Support, Day Care, and Educational Provision for Young Children
Volume 3	Family Placements
Volume 4	Residential Care
Volume 5	Independent Schools
Volume 6	Children with Disabilities
Volume 7	Guardians ad Litem and Other Court Related Issues
Volume 8	Private Fostering and Miscellaneous
Volume 9	Adoption Issues
Volume 10	Index

- *The Care of Children, Principles and Practice in Regulations and Guidance* (1991, London: HMSO)
- *Introduction to the Children Act 1989* (1991, London: HMSO)
- *Working Together to Safeguard Children* (1999, London: HMSO)
- *Assessing Children in Need and their Families* (2000, London: HMSO)
- *Framework for the Assessment of Children in Need and their Families* (2000, London: HMSO)
- *Initial and Core Assessment Records* (2000, London: HMSO)
- *Family Assessment Pack of Questionnaires and Scales* (2000, London: HMSO)

1.7 Official publications

- *Report of the Inquiry into Child Abuse in Cleveland*, 1987
- Home Office Circular 88/1982
- Home Office Circular 105/1982
- Home Office Circular 102/1988
- Home Office Circular 45/1991
- Local Authority Circular LAC (1988) 20
- Local Authority Circular LAC (1998) 29
- Local Authority Circular LAC (1999) 29
- *The Right to Complain* (Department of Health and Social Services Inspectorate, 1991, London: HMSO)
- *Guide to Listing Officers* (Lord Chancellor's Department, September 1991)
- *Guidance on Acting for Children in Private Law Proceedings Under the Children Act 1989* (Law Society Family Law Committee, 1994)
- *Guidance for Solicitors Attending Child Protection Conferences* (Law Society Family Law Committee, 1995)
- *Good Practice in Family Law on Disclosure* (Solicitors Family Law Association)
- *Guide – Acting for Children* (Solicitors Family Law Association, 2000)

1.8 Basic definitions

Interpretations of many terms used within the Children Act 1989 are given in s 105. The source of definitions created by other sections, other Acts or by case law and other sources are cited.

Adoption agency	Defined in ss 1(4) and 72(1) of the Adoption Act 1976 and includes local authorities and approved adoption societies but does not include foreign adoption agencies abroad.
Authorised person	(a) In care and supervision proceedings, and in child assessment orders, this means the NSPCC or its officers, under ss 31(9) and 43(13). A person (other than a local authority) may be authorised by order of the Secretary of State to bring proceedings under s 31 of the Act for a care or supervision order, but no one has been so authorised;

(b) in emergency protection orders, proceedings may be brought by an 'authorised officer' of the local authority, an 'authorised person' (as defined in (a) above), a 'designated' police officer or 'any other person'; see ss 31(9) and 44.

Authority	The local authority of a geographical area, including county councils, district councils, unitary authorities in England and Wales, Welsh county councils and Welsh county borough councils.
Care order	An order made under s 31(1)(a), placing a child in the care of a local authority. By s 31(11), this includes an interim care order made under s 38. By s 105, any reference to a child who is in the care of an authority is a reference to a child who is in their care by virtue of a care order.
Child	A person under the age of 18.
Child assessment order	An order under s 43 of the Act to produce the child and to comply with the court's directions relating to the assessment of the child. There are restrictions on keeping the child away from home under this section.
Child in care	A child in the care of a local authority pursuant to an order made under s 31(1)(a) or an interim order under s 38 of the Children Act.
Child in need	Under s 17, 'a child is taken to be in need if: (a) he is unlikely to achieve or maintain, or to have the opportunity of achieving or maintaining, a reasonable standard of health or development without the provision for him of services by a local authority;

(b) his health or development is likely to be significantly impaired or further impaired, without the provision for him of such services; or

(c) he is disabled.'

Also, see *Assessing Children in Need and their Families* (2000, London: HMSO) and *Framework For the Assessment of Children in Need and Their Families* (2000, London: HMSO).

Child minder	Defined in s 71 as a person who looks after one or more children under the age of eight, for reward; for total period(s) exceeding two hours in any one day. A person is not deemed to provide day care for children unless the total period(s) during which the children are looked after exceeds two hours in any day.
Child of the family	'[I]n relation to the parties to a marriage, means (a) a child of both of those parties, (b) any other child, not being a child who is placed with those parties by a local authority or voluntary organisation, who has been treated by both of those parties as a child of their family.'
Child looked after by a local authority	A child who is in the care of a local authority by virtue of a care order, or provided with accommodation by a local authority.
Child provided with accommodation by a local authority	A child who is provided with accommodation by a local authority in the exercise of its functions which stand referred to their social services committee under the Local Authorities Social Services Act 1970 (includes children in what was previously called 'voluntary care').

Children's home	Defined in s 63 as a home which usually provides or is intended to provide care and accommodation wholly or mainly for more than three children at any one time. Obviously, many homes contain three or more children and the section lists several exceptions, including the homes of parents, relatives, or those with parental responsibility for the children in question.
Community home	Defined in s 53 and may be '(a) a home provided, equipped and maintained by a local authority, or (b) provided by a voluntary organisation but in respect of which ... the management, equipment and maintenance of the home shall be the responsibility of the local authority; ... or the responsibility of the voluntary organisation'.
Contact order	Defined in s 8(1) as 'an order requiring the person with whom a child lives, or is to live, to allow the child to visit or stay with the person named in the order, or for that person and the child otherwise to have contact with each other'.
Development	Defined in s 31(9) as physical, intellectual, emotional, social or behavioural development.
Disabled	Defined in s 17(11) and 'in relation to a child, means a child who is blind, deaf, or dumb or who suffers from mental disorder of any kind or who is substantially and permanently handicapped by illness, injury or congenital deformity or such other disability as may be prescribed.
Education supervision order	Means an order under s 36(1) of the Act, putting the child with respect to whom the order is made under the supervision of a designated local education authority.

Emergency protection order	Under s 44 of the Children Act, this order:

'(a) operates as a direction to any person ... in a position to do so to comply with any request to produce the child ...

(b) authorises:

(i) the removal of a child to accommodation provided by or on behalf of the applicant, and his being kept there; or

(ii) the prevention of the child's removal from any hospital or other place in which he was being accommodated immediately before the making of the order; and

(c) gives the applicant parental responsibility for the child.'

(But also note – the exercise of parental responsibility under this order has limitations; see below, Chapter 6.)

Family assistance order	An order made under s 16 of the Act appointing a probation officer or an officer of the local authority to advise, assist and (where appropriate) befriend any person named in the order for a period of six months or less. Named persons may include parents, guardians, those with whom the child lives, or the child himself.

Family proceedings	In the Family Proceedings Court, all proceedings are treated as 'family proceedings' under s 92(2).

However, in other courts, 'family proceedings' are defined in s 8(3) and (4) as including any proceedings:

(a) under the inherent jurisdiction of the High Court in relation to children, including wardship but not applications for leave under s 100(3);

(b) under Pts I, II and IV of the Act; the Matrimonial Causes Act 1973; the Adoption Act 1976; the Domestic Proceedings and Magistrates' Courts Act 1978; Pt III of the

Matrimonial and Family Law Act 1996; also under ss 11 and 12 of the Crime and Disorder Act 1998;

(c) under s 30(8) of the Human Fertilisation and Embryology Act 1990, proceedings under s 30 of that Act are included.

Note that this definition does not include applications for emergency protection orders, child assessment orders or recovery orders.

Guardian	Means a guardian appointed under s 5 of the Act for the child, but not for the child's estate.
Guardian ad litem	An officer of the court with a duty to report to the court on the best course to be taken in the interests of the child. See ss 41–42, and the *Children Act Guidance* Vol 7.
Harm	Defined in s 31(9), meaning the ill treatment or the impairment of health or development. Where the question of whether the harm is significant or not turns on the child's health and development, his health or development shall be compared with that which could be reasonably expected of a similar child, s 31(10).
Health	Means physical or mental health.
Hospital	Any health service hospital, and accommodation provided by the local authority and used as a hospital. It does not include special hospitals, which are those for people detained under the Mental Health Act 1983, providing secure hospital accommodation.
Ill treatment	Defined in s 31(9) and includes sexual abuse and forms of ill treatment which are not physical.

Local authority	Means a council of a county, a metropolitan district, a London borough, or the Common Council of the City of London; in Scotland, it means a local authority under Social Work (Scotland) Act 1968, s 12.
Local authority foster parent	Means any person with whom a child has been placed by a local authority under s 23(2)(a) of the Act. Local authority foster parents may include a family; a relative of the child; or any other suitable person.
Local housing authority	Is as defined in the Housing Act 1944, meaning the district council; a London borough council; the Common Council of the City of London; or Council of the Isles of Scilly.
Parent	The natural (birth) mother or father of a child, whether or not they are married to each other at the time of the birth or of conception. The Children Act, when it says 'parent', means the birth parents of a child, including therefore natural fathers without parental responsibility. Where it intends to mean 'a parent with parental responsibility', it says so specifically.
Parent (in relation to adoption)	'[A]pplicants shall be the proposed adopter ... and respondents shall be each parent or guardian ... of the child,' r 15 of the Adoption Rules 1984 SI 1984/265.
	'Parent' has the same meaning as in the Children Act 1989. Sched, 10, para 30(7) of the Children Act provides an amendment to s 72(1) (interpretation) of the Adoption Act 1976 (to which the Adoption Rules are subordinate), that 'parent' shall mean 'any person who has parental responsibility for the child under the Children Act 1989' and 'parental responsibility'

and 'parental responsibility agreement' shall have the same meanings as under the Children Act 1989.

See *Re C (Minors) (Adoption: Residence Order)* [1994] Fam 1 and *M v C and Calderdale Metropolitan BC* [1993] 1 FLR 505, in which the Court of Appeal held that former parents would need leave to apply for s 8 orders after adoption since they are no longer 'parents' under the Children Act.

Parent with parental responsibility

All mothers have parental responsibility for children born to them.

Married fathers also have parental responsibility.

The father of a child who is not married to the mother is able to acquire parental responsibility in various ways under the Children Act. This term therefore excludes the natural father of a child who has not yet acquired parental responsibility under the Act.

Parental responsibility

Defined in s 3 and includes all the rights, duties, powers, responsibilities and authority which by law a parent of a child has in relation to the child and his property. It can be acquired by unmarried fathers in respect of their child by order or agreement under the Children Act, and by others through residence or guardianship orders, or by a local authority under a care order. Parental responsibility can be shared with others. It ceases when the child reaches 18, on adoption, death, or cessation of the care order.

Parental responsibility agreement

Defined in s 4(1) as an agreement between the father and mother of a child providing for the father to have parental responsibility for the child (a father married to the mother of their child at the time of the birth will automatically have parental responsibility for that child, but a father not so married will not). Format for the agreement is set out in the Parental Responsibility Agreement Regulations 1991 SI 1991/1478, as amended by SI 1994/3157.

Private fostering

See s 66: to 'foster a child privately' means looking after a child under the age of 16 (or if disabled, 18), caring and providing accommodation for him or her; by someone who is not the child's parent, relative, or who has parental responsibility for the child.

Prohibited steps order

Defined in s 8(1). Means an order that no step which could be taken by a parent in meeting his parental responsibility for a child, and which is of a kind specified in the order, shall be taken by any person without the consent of the court.

Protected child

A child protected under the Adoption Act 1976, that is, a child who is living with the applicant to adopt that child, who has given notice to the local authority of his or her intention to apply to adopt. The child is subject to the supervision of the local authority during the period of protection, which continues until one of a number of specified circumstances occur.

Registered children's home

Defined in s 63 as a home, registered under the Act, which provides (or usually provides or is intended to provide) care and accommodation wholly or mainly for more than three children, who are not siblings with respect to each other, at any one time. Section 63 provides a number of exceptions to the category of children's homes.

Relative	In relation to a child, this means a grandparent, brother, sister, uncle or aunt (whether of the full blood or of the half blood or by affinity) or stepparent.
Residence order	An order under s 8(1) settling the arrangements to be made as to the person with whom a child is to live.
Responsible person	Defined in Sched 3, para 1. In relation to a supervised child, it means: (a) any person who has parental responsibility for the child; and (b) any other person with whom the child is living.
Service	In relation to any provision made under Part III of the Act (local authority support for children and families), this means any facility.
Special educational needs	These arise when there is a learning difficulty which calls for special educational provision to be made. The Education Act 1981, s 1(1) sets out the meaning of 'learning difficulty'.
Specific issue order	An order under s 8(1) giving directions for the purpose of determining a specific issue which has arisen, or which may arise, in connection with any aspect of parental responsibility for a child.
Supervision order	An order under s 31(1)(b) and (except where express provision to the contrary is made) includes an interim supervision order made under s 38.

Supervised child/ supervisor	In relation to a supervision order or an education supervision order, these mean respectively the child who is (or is to be) under supervision and the person under whose supervision he is (or is to be) by virtue of the order.
Upbringing	In relation to any child, this includes the care of the child but not his maintenance.
Voluntary home	Means any home or other institution providing care and accommodation for children which is carried on by a voluntary organisation, with certain exceptions set out in s 60 of the Act.
Voluntary organisation	Means a body (other than a public or local authority) whose activities are not carried on for profit.

1.9　Orders available under the Children Act 1989

Order	Section	Maximum duration*
Parental responsibility	4	Age 18
Guardianship	5	Age 18
Residence	8	Age 16 (18 in exceptional circumstances)
Contact	8	Age 16 (18 in exceptional circumstances)
Prohibited steps	8	Age 16 (18 in exceptional circumstances)
Specific issue	8	Age 16 (18 in exceptional circumstances)
Family assistance	16	Six months
Care order	31	Age 18
Interim care order	38	First, not more than eight weeks; remainder, maximum four weeks

Supervision	31	Age 18; one year, may be extended to max total three years
Care contact order	34	Duration of care order
Education supervision	36	One year; repeatedly extensible for three years. Ceases at age 16
Child assessment	43	Seven days
Emergency protection	44	Eight days; extensible for further seven days

★ These orders may be brought to an end by court order, variation or discharge and subject to additional provisions. For details, please refer to the relevant chapter.

1.10 Introduction to the Children Act 1989

The Children Act 1989 came into force on 19 October 1991, containing 108 sections and 15 Schedules, and was accompanied by the Family Proceedings Courts (Children Act 1989) Rules 1991 SI 1991/1395; the Family Proceedings (Children) Rules 1991 SI 1991/910; and several volumes of *Guidance and Regulations* (listed above, 1.5).

The Children Act created a new unified court system consisting of three tiers: the High Court, the county court and the family proceedings court, each of which have concurrent jurisdiction and powers. Appeals from the family proceedings court go to the High Court, and from the county court and High Court to the Court of Appeal and the House of Lords. Cases may move up or down the tiers, transfers therefore being easier. The avoidance of delay is one of the underlying principles of the Children Act. To implement this the Act with its subsidiary rules created a new system of directions hearings to enable the courts to take firmer control of the timing of cases, admission of evidence and administrative matters.

The Children Act encourages families to stay together, imposing a duty on local authorities to provide services for children in need and their families, to reduce the necessity for children to be looked after away from home, and for child protection proceedings. Unless the criteria for the making of care or supervision orders are met, an order cannot be made. The courts, if concerned about the welfare of a child, may order a local authority to investigate the child's circumstances, but the courts have no power of their own volition to order a child into the care of a local authority.

The Children Act introduced a new concept of parental responsibility, which unmarried fathers may gain in relation to their children, and accessible to others, for example, grandparents or stepparents in conjunction with residence orders.

The Children Act creates orders governing aspects of a child's life, that is, contact with others; residence; and resolution of disputed aspects of child care – prohibited steps (forbidding actions) and specific issues (permitting actions to take place).

The powers of the police to act in a child's interests to remove and/or retain a child away from home are now limited to 72 hours.

The principles behind the Children Act and its guidance are that children are people whose rights are to be respected, not just 'objects of concern', and that children should wherever possible remain with their families, helped if necessary by provision of services, provided that their welfare is safeguarded. An atmosphere of negotiation and co-operation between professionals is encouraged. The welfare of the child is paramount, and, in the field of child care and protection, professionals are expected to work together in a non-adversarial way for the benefit of the child.

Section 6 of the Human Rights Act 1998 makes it unlawful for public authorities to act in ways incompatible with the Convention rights. This includes courts, tribunals and local authorities, including both acts and omissions (s 6). Those affected may bring proceedings or rely on the Convention (s 7) by way of an appeal, complaint or judicial review. Children Act proceedings and child protection generally are now subject to these provisions.

2 Principles Underlying the Children Act 1989

2.1 Paramountcy of the welfare of the child

The Children Act 1989 commences with a clear direction in s 1(1) that:

> When a court determines any question with respect to:
>
> (a) the upbringing of a child; or
> (b) the administration of a child's property or the application of any income arising from it,
>
> the child's welfare shall be the paramount consideration.

The court must have regard to the criteria set out in s 1(3) of the Children Act, known as the 'welfare checklist', in the circumstances set out below, 2.1.1.

2.1.1 The welfare checklist

(a) The ascertainable wishes and feelings of the child concerned (considered in the light of his age and understanding).

(b) His physical, emotional and educational needs.

(c) The likely effect on him of any change in his circumstances.

(d) His age, sex, background and any characteristics of his which the court considers relevant.

(e) Any harm which he is suffering or which he is at risk of suffering.

(f) How capable each of his parents, and any other person in relation to whom the court considers the question to be relevant, is of meeting his needs.

(g) The range of powers available to the court under this Act in the proceedings in question.

The court must have regard to the criteria set out in s 1(3) of the Children Act, known as the 'welfare checklist', when considering an application to vary or discharge an order under Pt IV of the Children Act (a child protection order) or a contested s 8 order for contact, residence, specific issue or prohibited steps.

The welfare checklist is not compulsory in other circumstances, but it is always useful for practitioners to consider it. If expert reports refer to these criteria whilst writing their reports, they ensure that they are complying with the principles of the Act.

There have been a number of cases in which the welfare checklist has been discussed. The welfare checklist has been held irrelevant in applications for leave to seek a s 8 order, where the criteria in s 10(9) apply. These are not substantive hearings under the Act (see *North Yorkshire CC v G* [1993] 2 FLR 732). However, if the child is the applicant for leave, then s 10(9) does not apply and the welfare principle is operative (*Re C (A Minor)* [1994] 1 FLR 96).

The guardian ad litem most often advises the court on the child's welfare in cases under Pt IV of the Act; see below, 15.1.

In private law cases (those between individuals as opposed to those involving State intervention in a family's life), the court may ask the court welfare officer to investigate the child's circumstances and to report back to the court the child's wishes and feelings, also advising the court on the best way to safeguard the child's welfare.

The court should be alert to any unusual circumstances or factors of concern in private law cases, even if the parties themselves are in agreement. The court may order a welfare officer's report, or direct the local authority to investigate a child's circumstances under s 37 of the Children Act, or make s 8 or s 16 (family assistance) orders of its own volition, if necessary.

In *Birmingham CC v H* [1994] 1 All ER 12; [1994] 1 FLR 224, the court held that in a Pt IV application concerning a child whose parent was herself still a minor, the welfare of the child subject to the application was paramount.

2.2   Delay is deemed prejudicial to child's interests

In any proceedings in which any question with respect to the upbringing of a child arises, the court shall have regard to the general principle that any delay in determining the question is likely to prejudice the welfare of the child (s 1(2) of the Children Act).

The court regulates the timing of cases by directions or preliminary hearings. In these, the court establishes who are parties to, or who should have notice of, the proceedings. The court ensures that the evidence is in order and service is carried out. A timetable is set for preparation and disclosure of evidence to other parties and the guardian ad litem, and a hearing date fixed. Directions given carry the force of court orders, failure to comply with them will be viewed by the court seriously and a full explanation for non-compliance will be required. Sanctions include wasted costs orders against those parties to a case who cause (or negligently allow) unnecessary delay. See *Ridelhalgh v Horsfield and Watson v Watson* [1994] 3 WLR 462; [1994] 3 All ER 848; [1994] 2 FLR 194 for the Court of Appeal's guidance on wasted costs.

2.3   No order unless necessary in the interests of the child

The Act assumes that the parties will do their best to resolve differences by negotiation and co-operation. Section 1(5) of the Children Act provides that the court has a positive duty not to make an order unless it is in the interests of the child to do so. This is referred to as the 'non-intervention' principle. See *Re W* [1994] 2 FCR 1216, in which the Court of Appeal discussed this principle in an application for a contact order.

3 Parental Responsibility

On 19 October 1991, ss 2 and 3 of the Children Act 1989 changed the status of parents in relation to their children, creating the concept of 'parental responsibility'.

Parental responsibility may be shared with others and it may be delegated in part, but it may not be surrendered or transferred entirely save by adoption. Each person who has parental responsibility may exercise it without a duty to consult others who also have it, with certain exceptions, but, for example, in the event of disagreement or a need for child protection, its exercise is also subject to orders of the court.

3.1 Definition, powers and duties of parental responsibility

Section 3(1) of the Children Act defines parental responsibility as:

> All the rights, duties, powers, responsibilities and authority which by law a parent of a child has in relation to the child and his property.

This wonderfully vague definition is not clarified anywhere in the Children Act except in s 3(2), which states that parental responsibility includes the powers of a guardian in looking after a child's property, for example, to give a valid receipt for a legacy. Paragraph 1.4 of the *Introduction to the Children Act 1989* (1991, London: HMSO) says: 'That choice of words emphasises that the duty to care for the child and to raise him to moral, physical, and emotional health is the fundamental task of parenthood and the only justification for the authority it confers.'

The Children Act 1989 Regulations and Guidance Vol 1 *Court Orders,* para 2.2, says that parental responsibility is concerned with bringing the child up, caring for him and making decisions about him, but does not affect the relationship of parent and child for other purposes. It does not affect rights of maintenance or succession.

Some statutory powers are reliant upon parental responsibility:

(a) appointment of guardian for a child in the event of death (Children Act, s 5(3));

(b) consent to the adoption of the child (Adoption Act 1976, s 16);

(c) access to the child's medical records (Access to Health Records Act 1990, ss 4, 5 and 12);

(d) consent to a child's marriage (Marriage Act 1941, s 1 as amended by Sched 12, para 5 of the Children Act);

(e) consent of all those with parental responsibility or leave of the court is required for removal of a child from the country, failing which a criminal offence is committed (Child Abduction and Custody Act 1985, s 1).

This provision applies even if there is a residence order in force, but under s 13(2) of the Children Act, the person holding a residence order in his or her favour may take the child abroad for holiday purposes for up to one month. The court may, of course, grant additional or general leave to take the child abroad for longer periods or permanently.

Other decisions and powers of those with parental responsibility include:

(a) Consent to medical assessment, examination or treatment.

See below, 3.1.2 and Chapter 12.

'Nearest relative' in the Mental Health Act 1983, s 27(2) is now amended to substitute for the word 'mother' both the mother and the father who has parental responsibility within the meaning of s 3 of the Children Act.

(b) Lawful correction. It is a defence to assault or to a charge of ill treating a child under s 1 Children and Young Persons Act 1933 for a parent to prove that the act was one of 'lawful correction'.

(c) Application for or veto of child's passport. *Practice Direction* [1986] 1 All ER 977, p 981 and *Re A* [1995] 1 FLR 767.

(d) Right to represent child as 'next friend' in all court proceedings where the child is a party except cases involving child protection or the upbringing of the child. The right can be removed if the parents act improperly or against the interests of the child (RSC Ord 80 r 2, CCR Ord 10 r 1).

(e) Right to name or re-name child. If both parents have parental responsibility and they agree, there is no problem. Please note *Practice Direction* [1995] 1FLR 458 and *Re PC (Change of Surname)* [1997] 2 FLR 730 for guidance. In cases where one parent wishes to change a child's name, the consent of all others with parental responsibility, or in the absence of consent, the leave of the court is required.

See, also, the Enrolment of Deeds (Change of Name) Regulations 1984 SI 1984/604.

Section 13(1) of the Children Act forbids name changes if a residence order is in force without consent of all those with parental responsibility for the child or leave of the court.

(f) Registration of a child's name. Under the Births and Deaths Registration Act 1953, a baby's name must be registered within 42 days of birth. Parents with parental responsibility may register the name. Fathers without parental responsibility, therefore, have no power to choose or register the baby's name without an order of the court. See *Re W, Re A, and Re B (Change of Name)* [1999] 2 FLR 930 and the comments of the House of Lords in *Dawson v Wearmouth* [1999] 1 FLR 1167 and [1999] 2 WLR 960.

(g) Right to decide child's education and duty to send their child to school, or to provide suitable alternative schooling, Education Acts 1962 and 1944. Sched 13, para 10 to the Children Act includes those who are not parents but who have parental responsibility for the child. See *Re Z (Minor) (Freedom of Publication)* [1996] 2 WLR 107; [1996] 1 FLR 191 on education, medical consent and publication of information.

(h) Decisions about a child's religion. The courts will not interfere unless the welfare of the child is threatened.

3.1.1 Duration

Parental responsibility lasts until a child is 18 years old if it belongs to the mother or the married father of the child, or to the father of the child by virtue of a parental responsibility agreement, legitimation or a court order. Parental responsibility can be acquired along with residence orders or guardianship. See below, 3.4.3 and 3.4.4.

3.1.2 Parental responsibility and medical consent

Save in emergencies, no person may be given medical treatment without consent. Whatever the motivation, this may constitute an assault for which practitioners may incur liability in tort or criminal law. Detention in hospital or any other place without consent could constitute false imprisonment. Those with parental responsibility, or a court, may give consent for medical assessment or treatment of a child. In emergencies, where there is no person capable or available to give or withhold consent, the doctor may lawfully treat the patient.

Medical records and notes should record who has parental responsibility for a child. With unmarried parents, in the absence of a parental responsibility agreement or court order, only the mother will have parental responsibility for the child. Should she (or any lone person with parental responsibility) die there will be no one with parental responsibility for the child. Single parents should therefore appoint a guardian for their child; see below, 3.4.4.

Young people aged 16 and over

Section 8 of the Family Law Reform Act 1969 confers on a person of 16 the right to give informed consent to surgical, medical, or dental treatment. Examinations or assessments could also impliedly be included. Those who suffer mental illness, disability, or psychiatric disturbance will be subject to the same mental health provisions and safeguards as adults.

Children aged under 16

See below, 12.1 and 12.2.

In *Gillick v West Norfolk and Wisbech AHA* [1986] AC 112, Mrs Gillick challenged her local health authority's provision of contraceptive advice to her daughters under 16 without her consent. The House of Lords supported the health authority's actions. In giving judgment, it formulated the concept known colloquially as '*Gillick* competence'. A child under 16 may make medical decisions according to her chronological age, in conjunction with mental and emotional maturity, intelligence, comprehension and the quality of the information provided to her.

In the case of *Re R (Minor: Consent to Medical Treatment)* [1992] Fam 11; [1992] 1 FLR 190, the Court of Appeal held that a '*Gillick* competent' child acquires a right to make decisions equal to that of each of his parents and only the absence of consent by all having that power would create a veto. If they cannot agree, then the doctor lawfully may act on consent of one. However, *A Guide to Consent for Examination or Treatment*, produced by the National Health Service Management Executive, advises that the refusal of an adult or competent young person must be respected.

If there is disagreement or refusal concerning medical treatment for a child when a doctor considers it necessary, and negotiation fails, then the matter can be resolved under s 8 of the Children Act by a specific issue order. The High Court in its inherent jurisdiction or under the Children Act can override the wishes of anyone in relation to medical treatment of a child in the child's best interests.

3.1.3 What if there is no one with parental responsibility?

Where immediate action is needed for the welfare of the child and no one with parental responsibility is available, s 3(5) of the Children Act provides that:

A person who:

(a) does not have parental responsibility for a particular child; but

(b) has care of the child, may ... do what is reasonable in all the circumstances of the case for the purpose of safeguarding or promoting the child's welfare.

This could apply to childminders, foster carers, neighbours and others looking after children who may need to take a child quickly to the GP or dentist, etc. This section, however, is not intended to cover consent for major medical issues.

3.2 Legal position of child's natural mother

Parental responsibility always belongs to a mother in relation to the children to whom she has given birth. It does not matter whether she is married to the father of the child (or to anyone else) or not. Nothing can remove that parental responsibility from her save death or adoption of the child.

3.3 Legal position of child's father

3.3.1 Married fathers

Under s 2(1) of the Children Act, a father automatically has parental responsibility for his children if he was 'married to their mother at the time of their birth'. This concept includes marriage at the time of the child's conception *Re Overbury (Deceased)* [1954] 3 All ER 308. The man must be the biological father. Section 1(2) of the Family Law Reform Act 1987 includes in the meaning of s 2(1) children legitimated by statute. This enables a child's father to gain parental responsibility if he subsequently marries the child's mother.

A married man has no parental responsibility for children who are not biologically his own, even if they are born during the marriage. Children born to a married couple as a result of artificial insemination will, however, be regarded as the child of the husband provided that the conditions set out in the Human Fertilisation and Embryology Act 1990 are met.

Note that men who become step-parents on marriage do not automatically acquire parental responsibility for their spouses' children, see below, 3.5.2.

3.3.2 Unmarried fathers

A father who is not married to the mother of his child has no parental responsibility, but he can acquire it in a number of ways. These are set out below.

3.4 Acquisition and loss of parental responsibility by child's natural father

3.4.1 Parental responsibility order

A father may apply under s 4(1)(a) of the Children Act for a parental responsibility order.

Applicant	The father (no one else can apply).
Parties/respondents	All those with parental responsibility (or if a care order is in force, those who had parental responsibility immediately prior to that order). On discharge application, all parties to the original proceedings. FPC(CA)R 1991 Sched 2 col (iii) and FPR 1991 App 3 col (ii).

Notice	Local authority providing accommodation for the child. Person(s) with whom the child is living at time of application, FPC(CA)R 1991 Sched 2 col (iv) and FPR 1991 App 3 col (iv). Person providing certified refuge for the child (see s 51 of the Children Act).
Status of child	With leave, a child of sufficient age and understanding can oppose the application or apply to set aside the order.
Procedural notes	Family proceedings under Children Act. Application on form C1 or C2 FPC(CA)R 1991 Sched 1 and FPR 1991 App 1. Service at least 14 days before date of directions/hearing. Respondents – copy application, date and time of directions/hearing. Notice – notification of application also date and time of hearing. The remaining procedure is the same as for s 8 applications, see below, Chapter 13.
Attendance	All parties shall attend, unless otherwise directed. The rules make an exception that proceedings shall take place in the absence of any party (including the child) if he is represented by guardian ad litem or solicitor, and it is in the child's interests having regard to the issues or evidence (FPC(CA)R 1991 r 16(2) and FPR 1991 r 4.16(2)).
Issues for the court	Degree of attachment between father and child; commitment shown by father to child; the reasons for the application (not improper or wrong). Children Act principles – welfare of child paramount; no delay; no order unless it is in best interests of child to make it.

Figure 1: Form from the Children (Parental Responsibility Agreement) Regulations 1991, as amended by SI 1991/1478 and SI 1994 /3157

the Child	Name
	Boy or Girl Date of birth Date of 18th birthday

Between the Mother	Name Address

and the Father	Name Address

We declare that we are the mother and father of the above child and we agree that the child's father shall have parental responsibility for the child (in addition to the mother having parental responsibility).

Signed (Mother)	Signed (Father)
Date	Date
Certificate of Witness — The following evidence of identity was produced by the person signing above:	The following evidence of identity was produced by the person signing above:
Signed in the presence of Name of Witness	Signed in the presence of Name of Witness
Address	Address
Signature of Witness	Signature of Witness
[A Justice of the Peace] [Justices' Clerk] [An Officer of the Court authorised by the Judge to administer oaths]	[A Justice of the Peace] [Justices' Clerk] [An Officer of the Court authorised by the Judge to administer oaths]

Relevant cases: *Re G (Minor) (Parental Responsibility Order)* [1994] 1 FLR 504; *Re T (Minor) (Parental Responsibility)* [1993] 2 FLR 450: *Re S (Parental Responsibility)* [1995] 2 FLR 648; *Re M (Contact: Family Assistance: McKenzie Friend)* [1999] 1 FLR 75; and *Re J (Parental Responsibility)* [1999] 1 FLR 784.

3.4.2 Parental responsibility agreement with the mother

The mother and father may agree that the father shall have parental responsibility for the child. The agreement must be made in accordance with the Children (Parental Responsibility Agreement) Regulations 1991, as amended; see SI 1991/1478 and SI 1994/3157.

The prescribed form is straightforward, and must be completed, signed by the mother and father and witnessed by a court officer or justices' clerk. Some courts ask the parents to produce the child's birth certificate, and evidence of their own identity incorporating their signature and photograph. (See Figure 1.)

3.4.3 Residence order and parental responsibility

A child's father may acquire a residence order under s 8 of the Children Act. This may be granted on application or of the court's own volition in the course of family proceedings, see below, Chapter 13.

The court has power to award parental responsibility with residence orders which subsists while the order remains in force. Residence orders expire by effluxion of time when the child reaches 16, unless there are exceptional circumstances, in which case it can be extended to age 18.

However, there are special provisions in the Children Act when the father of a child acquires a residence order relating to his child. On making the residence order, the court must also grant parental responsibility to the father, under ss 4 and 12(1) of the Children Act. The court shall not bring that parental responsibility order to an end whilst the residence order remains in force. The parental responsibility so granted will not expire with the residence order (for example, when the child reaches 16) but will last until the child is 18, unless the court specifically brings the father's parental responsibility to an end earlier, s 91(7) of the Children Act.

3.4.4 Guardianship

The court may appoint a guardian for a child under s 5 of the Children
Act where:

(a) there is no person with parental responsibility for the child; or

(b) a residence order has been made in favour of a parent or guardian
who died whilst the order was in force.

This parental responsibility subsists until the child reaches 18, unless
ended earlier by the court, s 91(7).

A parent with parental responsibility, or a guardian, may appoint a
guardian for a child in the event of his death under s 5(3) and (4) of the
Children Act respectively. If when he dies there is no one else alive with
parental responsibility, the appointed guardian will act. If there is anyone
with parental responsibility still alive, then the guardian will only be
able to act after the death of all others with parental responsibility. If,
however, someone with a residence order in her favour appoints a
guardian, she will act on the death of the appointer, in conjunction
with anyone else remaining alive who has parental responsibility.

3.5   Acquisition of parental responsibility
by others

3.5.1 Relatives

Relatives can obtain parental responsibility for a child along with a
residence order under ss 8 and 12(2) of the Children Act. Relatives
could also seek an appointment under s 5 as guardian of the child, which
automatically gives them parental responsibility until the child reaches
18 or the court orders otherwise, s 91(7).

A relative could also, in theory, apply to adopt a child in order to
gain parental responsibility. Courts will not usually favour adoption by
relatives because the effect of adoption is to sever legal ties with existing
parents and therefore may complicate family relationships, but in specific
circumstances it may be considered appropriate.

3.5.2 Stepparents

Stepparents do not acquire parental responsibility for the children of
their partners automatically on marriage. Currently, they can only

acquire parental responsibility along with a residence order under ss 8 and 12(2) of the Children Act, or by adoption.

The courts would not normally favour adoption by a step father unless the natural father is deceased, whether the natural father had parental responsibility or not, since adoption would sever his legal responsibility for, and relationship with, his child.

The mother of a child (who always has parental responsibility herself) may develop terminal illness or die whilst in a relationship with a man who is not the father of her child. The child may be very attached to him and he may be committed to the care of the child. If the mother dies, there are three possible scenarios:

(a) The child's genetic father is alive but has no parental responsibility.

The child will then legally have no one with parental responsibility.

Remedies:

- before the mother's death, the stepfather obtains a residence order alone or shared with the mother;

- mother appoints the stepfather guardian under s 5;

- if the mother has died, the stepfather obtains a residence order or guardianship order under s 5(1)(a). Guardianship automatically gives him parental responsibility until the child reaches 18 or the court orders otherwise, s 91(7).

(b) If the child's genetic father is alive and has parental responsibility.

The genetic father will then automatically hold the legal responsibility for the child.

The stepfather can seek a residence order. If he has been appointed as guardian by the mother before her death, this will only be effective immediately if she had a residence order in her favour before her death, s 5 (7)(b) of the Children Act. He could seek guardianship under s 5(1)(b) if the deceased mother had a residence order in her favour. In either case, he would have to share parental responsibility with the genetic father and resolve disputes by seeking an appropriate s 8 order. See below, Chapter 15 for discussion of s 8 orders.

(c) If the genetic father is dead, then there is no one with parental responsibility for this child.

The stepfather can seek a residence order under s 8 or guardianship under s 5(1)(a) of the Children Act. Guardianship automatically gives him parental responsibility until the child reaches 18 or the court orders otherwise, s 91(7).

The stepmother of a child, living with the child's father, would face similar problems on his death. The child's mother would always have parental responsibility. She would have a legal right to the care of the child unless otherwise agreed or ordered by the court. The stepmother could seek a residence order, or guardianship if the father had a residence order in force in his favour at the time of his death.

3.5.3 Non-relatives

Non-relatives may acquire parental responsibility with a residence order or through guardianship. The principles and comments outlined above, 3.5.2, apply. A local authority obtains parental responsibility for a child under s 31 of the Children Act with a care order, sharing it with the child's mother and anyone else who has it. The exercise by others of their parental responsibility in relation to the child may be limited by the local authority under the care order, but there should be partnership and co-operation. The local authority does not acquire parental responsibility when looking after children in voluntary arrangements.

4 Child Protection Procedures in Health and Social Work

Current child protection procedures are set out in a number of publications, the main ones being: *Working Together to Safeguard Children* (1999, London: HMSO, referred to below as *Working Together*) and the volumes of *Guidance and Regulations* made under the Children Act 1989, listed above, 1.5. These are all mandatory guidelines issued under s 7 of the Local Authority Social Services Act 1970. Local authorities must follow the guidance, and any departure from it must be justified in respect of any complaints procedure or judicial review. See below, Chapter 16.

Social work terminology and practice may vary in each area. It is important to know local procedures.

The Area Child Protection Committee (ACPC) is a multi-disciplinary group comprising senior representatives from all local child protection agencies. Its role is to organise and oversee the operation of child protection procedures in the locality. ACPCs each produce a local manual of guidance on policy and procedure. To obtain a copy, write to the local chair. A small fee to cover costs is usually payable. See *Working Together*, Chapter 4, for further information.

4.1 Hierarchy within social services departments

Below is a typical hierarchy of jobs within a social services child protection department. Terminology varies geographically. The head is the *Director of Social Services*, supported by several *Assistant Directors*, each of whom usually has an administrative responsibility related either to an area of work, or a geographical area. Social services departments are generally divided into task related divisions, for example, child care, community care, etc. One Assistant Director may have the responsibility for child care, which may or may not include adoption. Out in the field, the front line work is divided into geographical areas, headed by the *Divisional Manager* or *District Manager*. The work is carried out by social work teams, usually headed by a *Team Manager*, who is responsible for the management and supervision of the work of the social workers in her team.

Figure 2: Hierarchy within a social services department

SOCIAL SERVICES PERSONNEL CHART

Director of Social Services

Assistant Directors

Divisional Manager or District Manager

Child Protection Officer/Co-ordinator

Social work teams

Team Manager

Social workers

4.2   Referral procedures and preliminary investigations

See Chapter 5 of *Working Together* for guidance on referral procedures, and the flowchart of local authority referral procedures (opposite). The local ACPC must publish contact lists of addresses and telephone numbers. A member of the public concerned about a child should contact the police or social services. *Police* will usually either use their powers under s 46 of the Children Act in an emergency, or refer the matter to social services. Social services in each area appoint a 'duty officer' to take referrals. The *duty officer* will note the information given, ask further details to establish the name, whereabouts and circumstances of the child, and request information about the person making the referral if appropriate.

Professionals referring concerns to social services are usually required to confirm the referral in writing. This is to ensure that referrals are properly recorded, and not missed or, for other reasons, not followed up. A further safeguard against an inappropriate response or failure to respond to referrals is the child protection officer. His role is to oversee and note the progress of the referrals in his area, making sure that they are followed up appropriately and efficiently.

Figure 3: Flow chart of local authority referral procedures

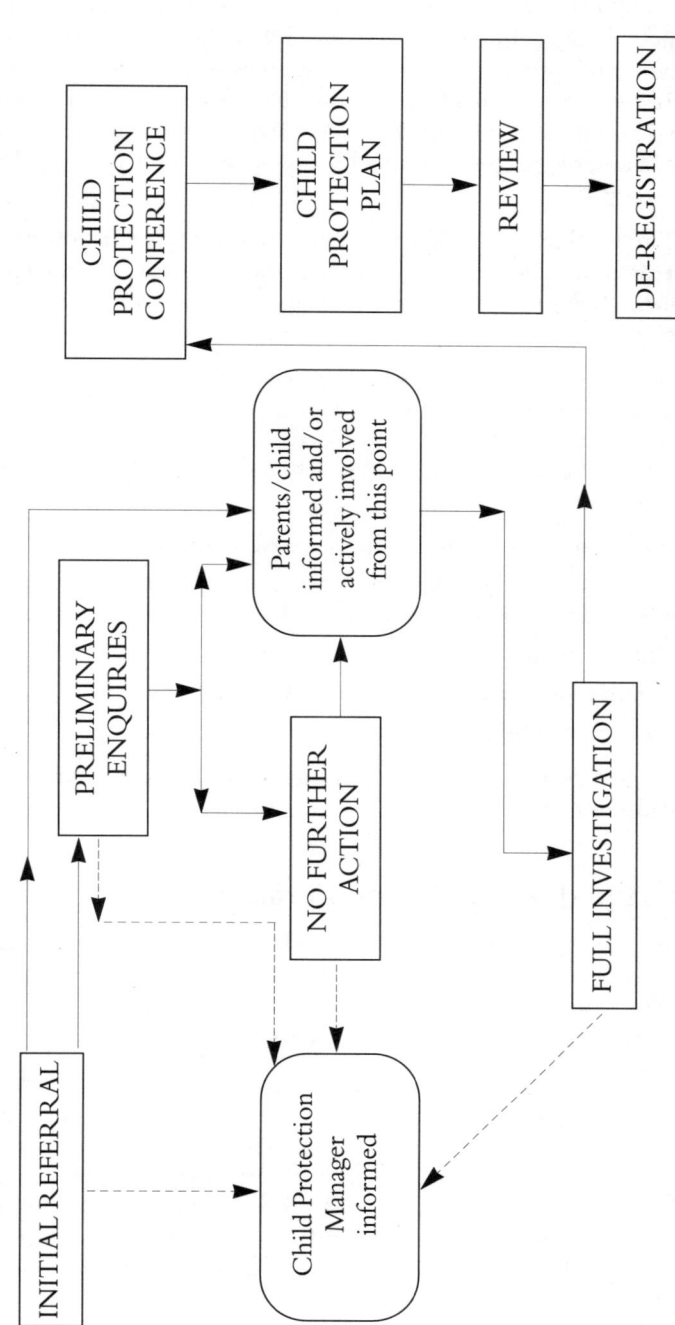

Note: court proceedings under the Children Act or criminal proceedings may run alongside these referral and registration procedures.

A child at risk of significant harm is, by definition, a child in need. In most cases, a child in need would remain at home, helped by the provision of appropriate services, resources and advice for the family. See below, Chapter 16. However, some children need greater protection. The local authority must therefore decide quickly whether it is necessary to seek emergency protection, child assessment or any other Children Act order.

The local authority immediately trawls for information from the referrer, police, general practitioner, and others to whom the family is known. *Working Together* encourages co-operation with parents in child protection:

> Whilst professionals should seek, in general to discuss any concerns with the family ... and seek their agreement to making referrals to social services, *this should only be done where such discussion and agreement-seeking will not place a child at increased risk of significant harm* [*Working Together*, para 5.6].

Possible outcomes of a preliminary investigation are:

(a) protection can be achieved by working in co-operation with the parents and provision of services, etc;

(b) child protection conference is required;

(c) urgent court proceedings are necessary;

(d) no further action needs to be taken.

Working Together, Chapter 5, sets out the options and inter-agency procedures in detail.

4.3   Child protection conferences

Working Together, in paras 5.53–5.104, offers guidance for child protection conferences. These are a multi-disciplinary meeting for discussion about the circumstances of a child held to establish whether the child's name should be placed on the child protection register.

If the conference decides to register the child, a social worker (key worker) is appointed for the family and a child protection plan is formulated by a core group of the agencies involved in discussion the family. A child protection conference is not a legal tribunal. It should not allocate blame, generate court action or assess s 31 criteria for a care application. It has only one decision to make: 'Is registration necessary?' The key worker fulfils statutory agency responsibilities, including development of the child protection plan, and is lead worker for the inter-agency work.

4.3.1 Function of child protection conference

Decision to be made

(a) Should child's name be entered on the *child protection register*?

(b) If *yes*, agree date for review – and also appointment of *key worker*.

(c) Establish the *core group* of professionals and family.

(d) Agree upon the *child protection plan* – agree upon the responsibilities of the core group members and family.

(e) Agreement on provision of resources for child/family by the agencies.

Figure 4: Process of child protection conference

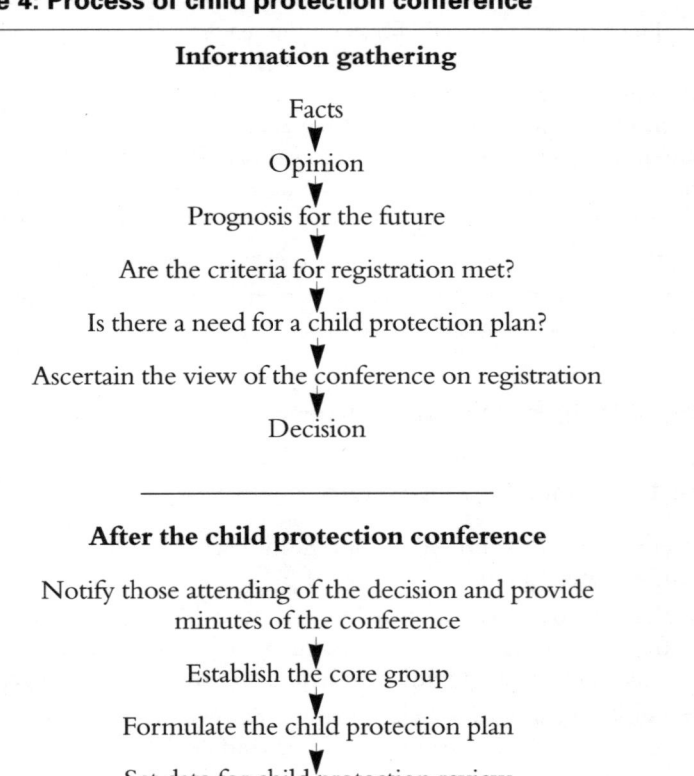

Information gathering

Facts

▼

Opinion

▼

Prognosis for the future

▼

Are the criteria for registration met?

▼

Is there a need for a child protection plan?

▼

Ascertain the view of the conference on registration

▼

Decision

———————————

After the child protection conference

Notify those attending of the decision and provide minutes of the conference

▼

Establish the core group

▼

Formulate the child protection plan

▼

Set date for child protection review

Child protection reviews should regularly follow registration at minimum intervals of six months. Extra reviews may be convened at the request of other professionals.

The chair is usually employed by social services, but independent, with no line–management responsibility for case work with the family involved. Attendance at child protection conferences is by invitation, which should include all professionals involved with the family, the parents and carers of the child and the child if of sufficient age and understanding. The chair should ensure that invitees are made welcome, and comfortable, with provision of refreshments, lavatories and other necessities. Minutes should be taken, and decisions recorded. Exclusions should be by the conference chair, and only when justified, for example, by a strong risk of violence. The chair is usually assisted by a minute taker, and may call upon specialist advice to assist on racial, ethnic, cultural, legal or religious matters, and psychologists or medical specialists where necessary.

The conference should focus on the needs of the child. Parents and older children may bring with them a supportive adult, whose role is to facilitate their comfort and expression of information and concerns to the conference. They may ask questions for clarification via the chair. Solicitors or legal staff may attend to support a child or parents, but not in an adversarial role, see the Law Society Family Law Committee's *Guidance for Solicitors Attending Child Protection Conferences in 1995.*

The provision of resources under s 17 and Sched 2 of the Children Act is a statutory duty for a child in need, see below, 4.6, and should not depend on registration.

4.4   Child protection register

4.4.1 Grounds for registration

There is, or is a likelihood of, significant harm leading to the need for a child protection plan (see below, 4.5). Either:

(a) there has been one or more identifiable incidents adversely affecting the child. These could be physical, sexual, emotional or neglectful, and professional judgment is that further incidents are likely; or

(b) significant harm is expected on the basis of professional judgment of findings of the investigation in this individual case, or on research evidence.

The conference will need to establish, as far as it can, the cause of, or likelihood of, the harm. This could apply to other siblings in the same household, justifying their registration. The category must be specified in each child's case.

4.4.2 Categories of abuse for registration

* Neglect

  Persistent or severe neglect of a child, failure to protect from danger, extreme failure to carry out aspects of care resulting in impairment of child's health or development, including non-organic failure to thrive.

* Physical injury

  Actual or likely physical injury to a child, failure to prevent physical injury or suffering, including deliberate poisoning, suffocation etc and Munchhausen's syndrome by proxy.

* Sexual abuse

  Actual or likely sexual exploitation of a child or adolescent. The child may be dependent and/or developmentally immature.

* Emotional abuse

  Actual or likely severe adverse effect upon the emotional or behavioural development of a child caused by persistent or severe emotional ill treatment or rejection. All abuse involves some form of emotional ill treatment. This category should be used where it is the sole or the main form of the abuse.

4.4.3 Criteria for de-registration

* Original factors no longer apply

  This will require a further conference to make the decision to de-register.

* Child and/or family moved permanently to another area

  Requirement that the new area has taken over the responsibility for future management of the case.

* Child no longer 'child' in the eyes of the law

  If a young person over 16 marries, or when he or she reaches 18, he or she is no longer a 'child' and therefore is not eligible for registration.

* The child dies.

4.5   Assessment of risk

See *Working Together to Safeguard Children* (1999, London: HMSO); *Framework for the Assessment of Risk* (2000, London: HMSO); *Assessing Children in Need and Their Families* (2000, London: HMSO); the range of *Initial and Core Assessment Records* for children of different age groups (2000, London: HMSO); and the *Family Pack of Questionnaires and Scales* (2000, London: HMSO). See, also, below, Chapter 16.

Local authorities on referral assess the likelihood of significant harm to a child, that is, evaluation of the potential risk to the child should she remain within her family, or the risk to the child if removed from home. After registration there should follow a carefully planned and structured comprehensive assessment within the child protection plan, to gain a better understanding of the child's situation.

Comprehensive assessments require co-operation of agencies and professionals involved with the family. Ask professionals involved about how long they will need, the venue, timing, and personnel to carry out the assessment: all must be clearly agreed.

4.6   Child protection plan

Child protection plans should not be confused with the care plans which are required in care proceedings; see below, Chapters 7 and 16.

Paragraphs 5.81–5.84 of *Working Together* recommend that there should be a written child protection plan made between family and professionals, in clear language, setting out the expectations and responsibilities of each party. Once the plan is agreed, each person should take responsibility to implement their part of it and to communicate with the others involved, with contingency provisions for crises and regular review. Parents and older children should have a copy of the plan, be informed of the nature and purposes of the interventions offered, and confirm that they agree with the plan and are willing to work with it. If the family have particular preferences about the protection work, which are not accepted by the professionals, then the professionals' reasons should be explained to the family, together with the right of the family to complain or to make representations.

4.7 Local authority duty to promote welfare of children in their area

Section 17 and Sched 2 to the Children Act 1989 impose on local authorities a duty to promote the welfare of children in their area, with special provision for 'children in need' (see below, 4.7.2), and children under five years old.

Local authorities must provide family centres as appropriate for children in its area with counselling advice or guidance, occupational, social or recreational activities, Sched 2, para 9(1) to the Children Act. Local authorities may provide recreational facilities, s 19(1) of the Local Government (Miscellaneous Provisions) Act 1976. Section 18 of the Children Act requires provision of day care for children under school age and for those of school age outside school hours or in the holidays. Section 17(6) of the Children Act authorises financial help in exceptional circumstances.

4.7.1 Duty to investigate potential or actual harm to child

Section 47 of the Children Act requires a local authority, when informed that a child who lives or is found in their area is subject to emergency or police protection, or has reasonable cause to suspect that the child is suffering, or is likely to suffer significant harm, to 'make such enquiries as they consider necessary to enable them to decide whether they should take any action to safeguard or promote the child's welfare'. See *Working Together*, paras 3.6–3.9, and *Working Together*, Chapters 5 and 6.

The enquiries are intended to establish whether the authority should make any application to the court or exercise their powers under the Children Act. The authority should consider providing accommodation for a child subject to an emergency protection order if they are not already doing so, s 47(3)(b); and, if the child is in police protection, then the authority should consider applying for an emergency protection order, s 47(3)(c). Enquiries include schooling. Refusal of access to the child or denial of information justifies an application for an emergency protection order. The local authority is under a duty to consider and timetable a review, if no present action is required. If action is necessary then the authority is under a duty to take it, s 47(8).

4.7.2 Duty to children in need

Section 17(1) of the Children Act imposes on local authorities a twofold duty:

>(a) to safeguard and promote the welfare of children within their area who are in need; and

>(b) ... to promote the upbringing of such children by their families,

>by providing a range and level of services appropriate to those children's needs.

Under s 17, those services are free to families on income support or family credit, but otherwise may be subject to means-related contributions.

Section 17(10) defines a child being in need if:

>(a) he is unlikely to achieve or maintain, or to have the opportunity of achieving or maintaining, a reasonable standard of health or development without the provision for him of services by the local authority ...;

>(b) his health or development is likely to be significantly impaired, or further impaired, without the provision for him of such services; or

>(c) he is disabled.

The services can be provided to the child direct, or to the family for the benefit of the child. Local authorities should publish information about the services in their area. Services are listed in Sched 2 to the Children Act.

'Health', 'development' and 'disabled' are all defined in the Children Act. The term 'disabled' was adopted to conform with the wording of the National Assistance Act 1948. Under s 17(6) of the Children Act assistance may be financial in exceptional circumstances, or in kind.

Services for children and their families

Schedule 2, para 8 of the Children Act lists services which local authorities should provide for children living with their families:

- advice, guidance and counselling;
- occupational, social, cultural, or recreational activities;
- home help (which may include laundry facilities);

- facilities for, or assistance with, travelling to and from home for the purpose of taking advantage of any other service provided under this Act or similar service (includes travel for contact purposes); and
- assistance to enable the child concerned and his family to have a holiday.

4.7.3 Duty to children under five

There is power under s 18 of the Children Act to provide day care for children under school age. *The Children Act 1989 Guidance Regulations* Vol 2 *Family Support, Day Care and Educational Provision for Young Children*, is helpful in giving ideas to practitioners about the nature and standards of the provision to be expected. Watch for new developments in day care and child minding issues, for example, policy on smacking.

4.7.4 Compliance with court order to investigate child's circumstances, s 37 of the Children Act

Under s 37 of the Children Act, in any 'family proceedings' in which a question arises as to the welfare of any child, if it appears to the court that it may be appropriate for a care or supervision order to be made, the court may order the local authority to investigate the child's circumstances. The local authority then has to consider whether they should apply for a care or supervision order, provide services for the family, or take any other action with respect to the child, s 37(2). If they decide not to seek an order, their reasons must be reported to the court within eight weeks, as must the services provided or to be provided, and any other action taken or proposed with respect to the child, s 37(3) and (4). The local authority may also need to review the situation and set a date for such a review, s 37(6).

5 Emergency Protection Orders

Emergency protection orders are available under s 44 of the Children Act 1989, as amended by the Family Law Act 1996, s 52, Sched 6, para 3. They are designed for situations when a child needs to urgent removal to a safe place; or to be retained in a safe place, such as a hospital. These orders may also be used to obtain access to a child in danger, when urgent action is necessary and/or to exclude a named person from a dwelling house or defined area in which the child lives, and they may include a power of arrest. An order may be made in respect of any child under 18 years of age living or found within the jurisdiction of the court.

5.1 Effects of order

The order gives parental responsibility for the child to the applicant, s 44(5). It authorises the applicant to remove, or retain the child, s 44(4)(b); and operates as a direction to anyone in a position to do so, to produce the child, s 44(4)(a). Under s 44(15) it is a criminal offence to obstruct the applicant in the exercise of his powers under the order.

The order has wide powers, and may contain any or all of these directions:

- authorising doctor, nurse, or health visitor to accompany the applicant to carry out the order, s 45(12) of the Children Act;
- for child to have contact with any named person, s 44(6)(a);
- for medical or psychiatric examination of the child, s 44(6)(b);
- requirement to disclose information concerning whereabouts of the child, s 48(1);
- authorisation to enter premises and search for the child, s 48(3);
- authorisation to search for another child in the same premises, s 48(4);

- issue of warrant to police officer to assist the applicant, s 48(9);
- authorisation for nurse, doctor, or health visitor to accompany police, s 48(11);
- exclusion requirement under s 44(A)(2) requiring a named person to leave and remain away from the dwelling house or area in which the child lives;
- undertaking in respect of an exclusion requirement s 44(B); and
- power of arrest in relation to an exclusion requirement s 44(A)(5) and (8).

5.2   Duration

Emergency protection orders last initially for eight days, renewable for a further seven days, s 45(1).

There are some exceptions to this general rule, including the following:
- if the order would expire on public holiday – first order goes to noon on the next day, s 45(2);
- if the child was in police protection (duration 76 hours maximum) before emergency protection order, and the designated police officer is the applicant on behalf of the local authority, the emergency protection order commences from beginning of police protection, s 45(3).

5.3   Grounds for application

The grounds to be proved depend upon who the applicant is.

Since anyone can apply for this order there is a general ground, which is that if the intention is to remove a child to a safe place, the applicant must satisfy the court that there is reasonable cause to believe that the child will suffer significant harm if not removed to accommodation provided by him, and also that there is suitable accommodation available for the child, s 44(1)(a)(i) of the Children Act.

If the applicant intends to retain the child in a safe place, then it must be proved that there is reasonable cause to believe that the child is likely to suffer significant harm unless retained in a safe place, s 44(1)(a)(ii). The grounds can be established on a prognosis, or based on past events indicating a future risk to the child. For the definition of 'significant harm', see below, 7.2 and 7.4.

A local authority applicant has an additional ground. It can satisfy the court that during s 47 of the Children Act enquiries about a child in its area, access to the child requested by a person authorised to seek it is being refused unreasonably, and that the access is required as a matter of urgency, s 44(1)(b)(ii) of the Children Act. See above, 4.7.1 for s 47 investigations. The question of reasonable refusal is a matter for the court. The *Children Act 1989 Guidance and Regulations* Vol 1 *Court Orders*, para 4.39, gives examples either way.

If the application is by an 'authorised person' (currently only the NSPCC), there is either the general ground, or an additional ground, that the applicant has reasonable cause to suspect that the child is suffering or is likely to suffer significant harm, that the applicant is making enquiries as to the child's welfare, that access to the child is being unreasonably refused, and access is urgently needed, s 44(1) of the Children Act.

The Children Act principles of the paramountcy of the welfare of the child, avoidance of delay and no order unless necessary for the welfare of the child apply. However, the application is not 'family proceedings' within the meaning of s 8(4) of the Children Act and so the 'welfare checklist' does not apply.

5.4   Practice and procedure

5.4.1 Application

Emergency protection orders may be sought by any person. Usually, the applicant is an 'authorised officer' of the local authority, or 'a designated officer' of the police.

The application should be made in the family proceedings court, unless the local authority has been directed to investigate under s 37, or there are proceedings pending in another court. In these exceptional cases the application can be made in the relevant court, Children (Allocation of Proceedings) Order 1991, Art 3. Application is on form C1, together with form C11. Procedure is governed by *Family Proceedings Courts (Children Act 1989) Rules 1991* (FPC(CA)R 1991) Sched 1 and *Family Proceedings Rules 1991* (FPR 1991) App 1 and r 4.4(4)(a). Applications for extensions should be made to the court which made the original order, Art 4. The application should name the child and, if this is not possible, it should give a description of the child for identification purposes.

A guardian ad litem will be appointed by the court to oversee the welfare of the child and to advise the court on the child's best interests, see ss 41–42 of the Children Act and below, 15.1.

5.4.2 Respondents

The forms of notice on form C6 plus a copy of the application, with the hearing date endorsed on it, must be served on respondents, together with notice of the date and place of the hearing.

Those listed below are automatically considered respondents to the application:

- everyone with parental responsibility for the child;
- if there is a care order, all those who had parental responsibility immediately prior to the care order;
- the child if of sufficient age and understanding.

See r 7(1), Sched 2 col (iii) FPC(CA)R 1991 and r 4.7(1), App 3 col (iii) FPR 1991. Others may be joined as respondents, and automatic respondents may be removed by direction of the court.

5.4.3 *Ex parte* applications

Application for an emergency protection order may be made *ex parte*, but first, in the family proceedings court, the leave of the justice's clerk or a magistrate must be obtained, r 4(4)(a) FPC(CA)R 1991 and r 4.4(4)(a) FPR 1991.

Applications may be made by telephone to the county court and High Court. The justices clerk may give leave for an *ex parte* application and directions concerning filing in the Family Proceedings Court.

5.4.4 Notice

If an application is made on notice, form C6A, and the date, time and venue of the application must be given within one day of the hearing to:

- parents of the child without parental responsibility;
- any person caring for the child or with whom the child is living when the proceedings are commenced;
- a local authority providing accommodation for the child;
- a person providing a refuge under s 51 of the Children Act, in which child lives.

See r 4(1)(b) and Sched 2 col (iv) FPC(CA)R 1991; r 4.4(1)(b) and App 3 col (iv) FPR 1991.

5.4.5 Service

Service must be effected one day before the directions or application hearing, r 4.4(1)(b), Sched 2 FPC(CA)R 1991 and r 4.4.4.(1)(b), App 3 FPR 1991.

5.4.6 Attendance

By r 16(2) FPC(CA)R 1991 and r 4.16.2 FPR 1991, the parties and/or their legal representatives have to attend directions appointments and hearings unless otherwise directed by the court. If respondents fail to appear, the court may proceed in their absence. If applicants fail to attend, the court may refuse their application, rr 16(5) and r 4.16(5).

5.5 Contact, accommodation and the rights of the child

5.5.1 Contact

The child must be allowed reasonable contact with:

*   parents;
*   those with parental responsibility for the child;
*   anyone with whom the child was living before the order;
*   anyone with a contact order under s 8 or s 34 in force in respect of the child, or anyone acting on their behalf;
*   anyone with an order for access to the child, s 44(13) of the Children Act.

The court can control the contact by directions within the emergency protection order. See s 44(13)(dd) and (6)(a) and Sched 14, para 9(4) of the Children Act.

The Care of Children, Principles and Practice in Guidance (*Principles and Practice*), paras 14–16, is relevant to contact issues. See also *Guidance and Regulations* Vol 4 *Residential Care,* paras 2-5–2-6.

5.5.2 Accommodation

The child has the right to accommodation provided, funded or arranged by the local authority and which meets the standards set by *Residential Care*, by the Arrangements for Placement of Children Regulations 1991 and by Sched 2 to the Children Act.

5.5.3 Rights of the child

The child has the right to be returned to his home once the danger has passed and the grounds for the order no longer subsist, s 44(10) of the Children Act.

A child of sufficient age and understanding has the right to be consulted and informed about events that are happening, see *Residential Care,* paras 2.20(c), 2.21 and 2.10–2.12.

The emergency protection order may include a direction about medical or psychiatric assessment of the child, s 44 of the Children Act. The directions can order or prohibit examinations, either completely or without leave of the court. Directions for examination/assessment can include venue, personnel to be present, and nomination of the person(s) to whom results should be given. A child of sufficient age and understanding has the right to make an informed refusal of medical or psychiatric assessment. A '*Gillick* competent' child, or a young person over 16, may consent to or refuse medical treatment, see below, 12.1 and 12.2.

5.6   Variation and discharge

There is no right of appeal against an emergency protection order, perhaps because of its short duration. It can be challenged by an application to vary or to discharge the order.

The child, child's parents, those with parental responsibility for the child, and anyone with whom the child was living when the order was made, can make an application for variation or discharge, s 45(8) of the Children Act.

The rules provide, however, that if a person has had notice of the original application for the emergency protection order, and has attended and opposed the application at the hearing, then there is no right to seek a discharge, s 45(11) of the Children Act. There has to be a time lapse of 72 hours after the order is made before there can be a hearing of an application for discharge, s 45(9) of the Children Act.

6 Child Assessment Orders

6.1 Effects of order

Child assessment orders were created by s 43 of the Children Act 1989. Note that, in *The Children Act 1989 Guidance and Regulations* Vol 1 *Court Orders*, para 4.11, it is suggested that a child assessment order application may follow a s 47 investigation. It enables the local authority to discover sufficient information about the child to plan appropriate action in the child's interests. Paragraph 4.9 considers this order appropriate 'where the harm to the child is long term and cumulative rather than sudden and severe'. It is appropriate where there is no emergency necessitating removal of a child from home for protection, but the parents or carers of the child are demonstrably failing to co-operate with the local authority in facilitating an assessment. The order can stipulate the nature of the assessment sought, the venue and duration, the person(s) to whom the results are to be given, and the contact between the child and others during the subsistence of the order.

6.2 Grounds for application

The court may, by s 43(1) of the Children Act, make the order only if it is satisfied that:

- the applicant has reasonable cause to suspect that the child is suffering, or is likely to suffer significant harm;
- an assessment of the child's state of health or development, or of the way in which he is being treated, is required to enable the applicant to determine whether or not the child is suffering or is likely to suffer significant harm; and

- it is unlikely that such an assessment will be made, or be satisfactory, in the absence of an order under this section.

6.3   Practice and procedure

6.3.1 Application

Application can only be made by a local authority or authorised officer (this category currently only includes the NSPCC), see ss 43(1) and (13) and 31(9) of the Children Act. It should be on form C1 together with form C16. It must be determined at a full court hearing. Under s 91(15) of the Children Act, no further applications may be made without leave in a six month period following disposal of the first application.

6.3.2 Venue

Under the Children (Allocation of Proceedings) Order 1991 SI 1991/1677, the application should be made in the Family Proceedings Court unless there are pending proceedings in another court or the application is the result of a court direction to investigate under s 37 (see above, 4.7.4).

6.3.3 Respondents

Notice on form C6, plus a copy of the application with the date, time and place of hearing, must be served on those listed below who are automatically regarded as respondents to the application.

These include:

(a) everyone with parental responsibility for the child;

(b) the child, if of sufficient age and understanding;

(c) where there is a care order, everyone with parental responsibility before the making of the care order. See Sched 2 col (iii) of the FPC(CA) 1991 and App 3 col (iii) of the FPR 1991.

Others may be joined as respondents, and automatic respondents may be removed by order of the court, r 7(1) FPC(CA) 1991 and r 4.7(1) FPR 1991.

6.3.4 Notice

Notice of the proceedings on form C6A and the date, time and venue of the application must be given to those entitled, including:

(a) parents;

(b) those with parental responsibility for the child;

(c) any person caring for the child or with whom the child is living;

(d) anyone entitled to contact with the child under a contact order under ss 8 or 34 of the Children Act (or former access order);

(e) a local authority providing accommodation for the child;

(f) a person providing a refuge in which the child lives under s 51 of the Children Act;

(g) the child, if of sufficient age and understanding.

See r 4(3), Sched 1 and Sched 2 col (iv) FPC(CA)R 1991 and r 4.4(3) and App 3 col (iv) FPR 1991.

6.3.5 Service

Service must be seven days before the directions or application hearing, rule 4.4(1)(b), Sched 2 FPC (CA) 1991 and App 3 FPR 1991.

6.3.6 Generally

The principles in s 1 of the Children Act (see above, Chapter 2) apply to s 43 applications, save that the welfare checklist does not apply.

Section 8(4)(a) of the Children Act defines 'family proceedings', and within these proceedings the court has power to make other orders of its own volition. Section 43 orders are not 'family proceedings'. This means that the court can only make or refuse the order sought, or treat the application as one for an emergency protection order instead, s 43(3). The court must not make a child assessment order if in all the circumstances of the case the court considers an emergency protection order more appropriate, s 43(4).

The duration of the order is limited to seven days from the date specified for commencement, s 43(5). The Act does not state that the seven days must be consecutive, but there seems no other practicable interpretation. It cannot be extended and, unless the court grants leave, it cannot be renewed until a six month period has elapsed, s 91(15) of the Children Act.

6.3.7 Discharge of order

On an application for discharge of a child assessment order, the case will be listed for directions. The procedure is the same as an application for an original order.

6.4   Contact, accommodation and the rights of the child

6.4.1 Contact

There are no specific rules as to contact, but it is submitted that the comments in *The Care of Children, Principles and Practice in Regulations and Guidance*, paras 14–16 and *Guidance and Regulations* Vol 4 *Residential Care* paras 2–5–2–6 relevant to contact with a child in care are applicable to this situation. This would mean that the child should be allowed reasonable contact with:

(a) parents;

(b) those with parental responsibility for the child;

(c) anyone with whom the child was living before the order;

(d) anyone with a contact order under ss 8 or 34 in force in respect of the child, or anyone acting on their behalf;

(e) anyone with an order for access to the child, s 44(13) of the Children Act.

The court can control contact by directions within the child assessment order. See s 43(10) of the Children Act. Note the operation of Art 8 of the Human Rights Act 1998 (right to family life) as it may affect a child's right to contact with family and siblings.

6.4.2 Accommodation

The child has the right, if removed from home, to reside in accommodation provided, funded or arranged by the local authority which meets the standards set by *Residential Care*, by the Arrangements for Placement of Children Regulations 1991 and by Sched 2 to the Children Act.

6.4.3 Rights of the child

A child of sufficient age and understanding has the right to be consulted and informed about events that are happening; see *Residential Care,* paras 2.20(c), 2.21 and 2.10–2.12.

The child assessment order will usually include a direction about medical or psychiatric assessment of the child. Examinations can be ordered or prohibited. Directions can include venue, personnel to be present, and nomination of the person(s) to whom results of assessments etc should be given. A child of sufficient age and understanding has the right to make an informed refusal of medical or psychiatric assessment, s 43(8) of the Children Act. A '*Gillick* competent' child, or a young person over 16, may consent to or refuse medical treatment. See below, 12.1 and 12.2.

A child should only be kept away from home where it is absolutely necessary for assessment purposes, and in accordance with directions in the order, s 43(9)(b) and (c) of the Children Act.

6.5 Appeals, variation and discharge

Appeal lies against the making or refusal of a child assessment order, from the Family Proceedings Court to the High Court and from the county court or High Court to the Court of Appeal.

Applications to vary or discharge the order may be made on form C1, with two days' notice, to the court which made the original order. See Art 4, Children (Allocation of Proceedings) Order 1991.

Contraventions of the Human Rights Act may be dealt with by complaint, judicial review or appeal against a court order.

7 Care and Supervision Proceedings

The Children Act 1989 is referred to as the 'Children Act', and all sections cited below are from the Children Act unless otherwise stated.

7.1 Care order – definitions

Care orders are those orders made under s 31 placing a child into the care of a designated local authority. The *designated local authority* is the local authority for the area in which the child resides, or within whose area any circumstances arose in consequence of which the care order is being made.

A *child* is a person under the age of 18, s 105(1). The term *care order* includes an *interim care order* made under s 38. Reference to a *child in care*, means a child subject to a care order, and not a child looked after by the local authority under a voluntary arrangement.

7.2 Grounds for application for a care or supervision order

A care order cannot be made in respect of a child over 17 years old, or 16 if married, s 31(3).

Under the Children Act there is only one route into statutory care. The court must be satisfied that the criteria set out in s 31 are met and also that an order is necessary for the welfare of the child.

The underlying principles in s 1(1), (2) and (5) – the paramountcy of the welfare of the child, avoidance of delay and no order unless necessary – all apply. The court must have regard to the welfare checklist in s 1(3), see Chapter 2 above.

Section 31(1) specifies the grounds for application for a care or supervision order:

(a) that the child concerned is suffering, or likely to suffer, significant harm; and

(b) that the harm; or likelihood of harm, is attributable to:

   (i) the care given to the child, or likely to be given to him if an order were not made, not being what it would be reasonable to expect a parent to give to him; or

   (ii) the child's being beyond parental control.

Definitions from s 31(9):

Harm	Ill treatment or the impairment of health or development.
Development	Means physical, intellectual, emotional, social or behavioural development.
Health	Includes physical or mental health.
Ill treatment	Includes sexual abuse and forms of ill treatment which are not physical.

7.3 Significant harm

The difficult part for practitioners in care and supervision proceedings is often the definition and proof of 'significant harm'. Section 31(9) gives the definitions (see above). It is also provided in s 31(10) that: 'Where the question of whether harm suffered by a child is significant turns upon the child's health or development, his health or development shall be compared with that which could reasonably be expected of a similar child.' The court will therefore have to compare this particular child with a notional similar child, of similar background, age, ethnicity, culture, race, religion and physique.

Significant Harm (Adcock, M, White, R and Hollows, A, 1991, London: Significant) gives useful information from a variety of medical and psychological perspectives about the assessment of harm. The reader is led step by step through a logical process of evaluating whether the successive stages of the threshold criteria are met. It helps in case preparation and effective evidence gathering, and assists in explaining the criteria to the court (see Figure 5, p 65).

Significant harm must be attributable to parental care falling below a reasonable standard, or the child being beyond parental control. The test is objective, measured against a reasonable standard of parenting.

In *Re M (Minor) (Care Order)* [1994] 3 All ER 298 HL; [1994] 2 AC 424; [1994] 3 WLR 558; [1994] 2 FLR 577 the House of Lords held that 'is suffering' means at the date of the hearing, or at the moment when the child was initially protected, provided the protection is uninterrupted until the date of the hearing. A careful reading of this judgment is recommended. Whilst the court may find the grounds proved, it may also take account of the circumstances prevailing at the hearing date in considering whether it is necessary to make an order, and which order would be most appropriate.

7.3.1 Standard of proof

Significant harm must be established on a balance of probabilities. In *Re P (Minor) (Care Proceedings)* [1995] 1 FCR 583 the court held that the more serious the allegation, the more convincing the evidence needed to tip the balance.

'Likely to suffer' has been interpreted by the House of Lords to mean 'a real possibility, a possibility that cannot sensibly be ignored having regard to the nature and gravity of the feared harm in the particular case', see *Re H and Others (Child Sexual Abuse: Standard of Proof)* [1996] 1 All ER 1, [1996] 1 FLR 80,

This was an application was for a care order in respect of four children, based on an allegation of sexual abuse (by the father) of the oldest child, and therefore a likelihood of significant harm to the younger three. The House of Lords confirmed that the s 31(2) criteria was not met in the case of the oldest child, leaving no power to go on and consider the likelihood of harm to the younger three children.

7.4   Practice and procedure

7.4.1 Applicants

Only a local authority or authorised person may apply for a care order, s 31(1). An 'authorised person' at the moment is an officer of the NSPCC, s 31(9).

The court has no power to make a care order without an application, but under s 38(1) it may make an interim care or supervision order on adjouring an application for a full order; or alongside making a direction to the local authority to investigate the child's circumstances under s 37.

7.4.2 Venue

Applications should be made in the Family Proceedings Court, unless one of three exceptions apply: there has been a court directed investigation under s 37 of the Children Act; there are pending proceedings; or the application is to extend, vary or discharge an existing order. In these exceptional cases, the application may be made in the same court as the other proceedings, Children (Allocation of Proceedings) Order 1991, Art 3.

County courts are divided into divorce centres, care centres and family hearing centres. Care and supervision applications must be heard in care centres. Refer to the *Family Proceedings (Allocation to Judiciary) Directions 1993* [1993] 2 FLR 1008.

It may be appropriate for a care or supervision application to be heard in a higher court. Transfers are governed by *the* Children (Allocation of Proceedings) Order 1991 SI 1991/1677; and the Children (Allocation of Proceedings, Appeals) Order 1991 SI 1991/1801 and the Family Proceedings (Amendment) Rules 1991 SI 1991/2113; also, Home Office Circular 45/91. Here there is space only to summarise these provisions, and to draw attention to potential pitfalls which may be encountered. Under Children (Allocation of Proceedings) Order 1991, Art 21, if the procedural requirements are broken, proceedings are not invalidated nor is it ground for appeal.

Certain cases should be heard in the High Court: post-adoption contact applications; specific issue on medical matters; HIV test for a child; injunctions concerning publicity; and applications by a child for leave to apply for a s 8 order. See Chapter 14; *Practice Direction* [1993] 1 WLR 313 and 1 All ER 820; and the Children Act Advisory Committee Transfer Trigger List (below, 14.3).

7.4.3 Form

Application must be made on form C1 (or C2 if made in existing proceedings) with form C13.

7.4.4 Respondents

Notice of proceedings with date and place of hearing, together with a copy of the application endorsed with the date of the hearing or directions, must be served three days before the hearing on those listed below who are automatically considered respondents to the application:

(a) everyone with parental responsibility for the child;

(b) the child, if of sufficient age and understanding.

See rr 4 and 7(1) and Sched 2 col (iii) FPC(CA)R 1991 and rr 4.4 and 4.7(1), App 3 col (iii) FPR 1991. Others may be joined as respondents and automatic respondents may be removed by direction of the court.

7.4.5 Notice

Notice on form C6A, with the date, time and venue of the application must be served three days before the hearing on:

(a) parents without parental responsibility for the child;

(b) any person caring for the child or with whom the child is living;

(c) a local authority providing accommodation for the child;

(d) a person providing a refuge in which child lives under s 51;

(e) any person who is party to relevant proceedings in respect of the child.

See r 4(3), Sched 1 and Sched 2 col (iv) FPC(CA)R 1991 and r 4.4(3) and App 3 col (iv) FPR 1991.

7.4.6 Service

Service on those entitled to notice, or on respondents, must be three days before the directions or application hearing, r 4.4(1)(b), Sched 2 FPC(CA)R 1991 and App 3 FPR 1991. The court can dispense with the requirements of service *Re X (Care: Notice of Proceedings)* [1996] 1 FLR 186. The welfare principle does not apply in consideration of service since it is not a substantive application.

7.4.7 Attendance

Proceedings must take place in the child's absence if the court considers this in his interests, having regard to the matters to be discussed or the evidence likely to be given, and he is represented by a solicitor, r 16 FPC(CA)R 1991 and r 4.16 FPR 1991.

By the same rule, the other parties and/or their legal representatives have to attend directions appointments and hearings unless otherwise directed by the court. If respondents fail to appear, the court may proceed in their absence. If applicants fail to attend the court may refuse their application, r 16(5) and r 4.16(5). Directions hearings are used by the court to oversee the timing of the case, the filing and service of evidence, and the appointment of parties and the guardian ad litem. For discussion of the use of directions hearings and case preparation, see Chapter 11 below.

7.5 Interim orders

On adjourning a care or supervision application, the court has the power to make an interim order when satisfied that there are reasonable grounds for believing the circumstances justifying a care order exist, s 38(2). An interim order's maximum duration is an initial maximum of eight weeks, followed by extensions of up to four weeks each. Shorter interim orders are possible, s 38(4) and (5).

(a) The initial interim order may be up to eight weeks.

(b) If the initial order is less than eight weeks, then the second interim order must be no more than a total of eight weeks less the duration of the initial interim order (for example, first order five weeks, second order three weeks; or first order two weeks, second six).

(c) Any subsequent orders must be of no more than four weeks' duration.

The Act seeks to avoid delay in dealing with cases. Courts will not permit repeated interim orders.

On making an interim order, directions may require medical or psychiatric examination or assessment of the child, which a child of sufficient understanding may refuse, s 38(6). (See Chapter 12, below, for the rights of children.) Directions may also prevent the abuse of children by repeated examinations, s 38(7). Directions may also govern the time and venue of the examination, who shall be present and to whom the results will be given.

7.6 Effects of care order

7.6.1 Duration

A care order subsists until the child reaches 18, unless brought to an end earlier by the court, s 91(1) and (12).

It will cease on the making of:

(a) an adoption or a freeing order, Adoption Act 1976, ss 12(3) and 18(5);

(b) a residence order, Children Act, s 91(1);

(c) the making of a supervision order in substitution for a care order, Children Act, s 39(4);

Figure 5: Significant harm flow chart

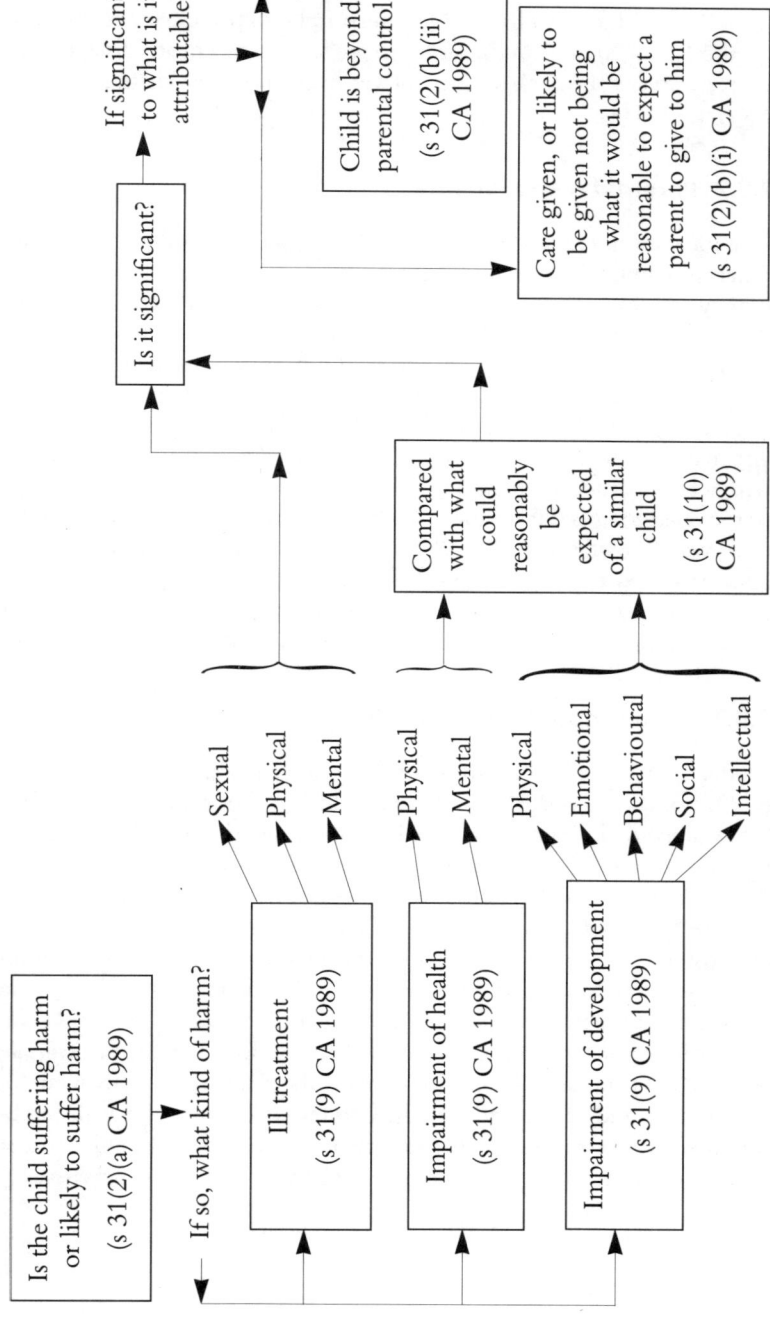

(d) the making of an order for discharge of care, Children Act, s 39(1);

(e) if the child goes to live in Northern Ireland, the Channel islands or the Isle of Man then the order may cease to be enforceable, but the regulations about this have not yet been made under the Children Act, s101(4).

7.6.2 Parental responsibility

The local authority acquires parental responsibility under a care order, sharing it with those who already have it. The local authority may, however, limit the exercise of parental responsibility by others whilst the care order subsists, s 33(3). There are limits on the powers of the local authority during a care order. They may not change a child's religion; consent to his adoption; or appoint a guardian for the child, s 33. The parental responsibility which others had when the care order was made still subsists, but it cannot be exercised in a way which conflicts with a court order, s 2(6) and (8). The child's name may not be changed or the child removed from the United Kingdom without written consent of all with parental responsibility or leave of the court, s 33(7). The local authority may remove the child from the jurisdiction of the court for up to one month, and under Sched 2, para 19, the local authority can make arrangements for a child to live abroad, with certain restrictions.

7.6.3 Accommodation of the child

Under s 33(1), the local authority has a duty to receive the child into its care once the order is made. The child is the responsibility of the local authority, and it must provide for somewhere to live and maintenance for the child, s 23(1). The child may remain at home. *The Children Act 1989 Guidance and Regulations* Vol 4 *Residential Care* (*'Residential Care'*) and Vol 3 *Family Placements* govern the placements of children in residential and foster care and placements with their family. There is a duty on the local authority to keep children with their birth family if at all possible, consistent with their welfare, and *The Care of Children, Principles and Practice in Regulations and Guidance* (1991, London: HMSO) (*'Principles and Practice'*) paras 5, 8, 9 and 10 emphasise the importance of maintaining family links and of the primary duty to try to keep a child at home by the provision of resources. A care order and removal of a child is seen as the last resort, and in itself 'a risk to be balanced against others', para 8.

7.6.4 Contact with a child in care

Paragraphs 2.6 and 6.26 of *Residential Care* assume that contact with its family is in the best interests of a child in care unless proved otherwise. Parents and others in financial or practical difficulty should receive help with travelling to contact sessions, Sched 2, para 16.

Contact with children in care is subject to the control of the court. This is different from contact in private law, and orders available under s 34 are referred to as 'care contact orders'. The Act requires that children looked after by a local authority under a care order will be afforded 'reasonable contact' with those people listed in s 34(1). They are:

(a) parents;

(b) guardians;

(c) anyone with a residence order in force immediately before the care order was made;

(d) anyone with care of the child under a High Court order made under its inherent jurisdiction.

The court may, on the application of the guardian ad litem or the child, make whatever order it considers appropriate in respect of contact between the child and any named person. Where the child or the local authority is the applicant, the scope of the order is very wide. On the application of any person entitled to contact under s 34(1) (those listed above), or anyone else with leave of the court, a care contact order may be made.

When the court makes a care order, it may make a care contact order if necessary in the interests of the child, s 34(5). The forms, those entitled to notice and respondents, are the same as for the care order, save that the period of notice is three days, see r 4(1)(b) FPC(CA)R 1991 and r 4.4(1)(b) FPR 1991.

In urgent cases, if necessary, a local authority may stop contact for up to seven days, s 34(6). If it wishes to stop contact for longer, it must apply to the court for a care contact order under s 34, authorising contact with a named person to be curtailed or to be refused. It is argued that severe curtailment of contact is tantamount to a refusal within the meaning of s 34 since the section refers to 'reasonable contact' and the court is the ultimate arbiter of reasonableness.

7.6.5 Rights of the child in care proceedings and under a care order

A child in care has rights which are protected by the Human Rights Act 1998, the Children Act and also by the guidance issued under it. The child has a right to:

(a) refuse medical or psychiatric assessment ordered within an interim care order under s 38(6) of the Children Act;

(b) contact with his or her family (see 7.6.4 above) and *Principles and Practice* paras 9 and 13–16;

(c) consultation on issues involving her care (see Family Placements, paras 2.21 and 6.4; also, *Residential Care*, paras 2.21 and 2.45; ss 22(4), 61 and 64 of the Children Act; para 25 *Principles and Practice*);

(d) information about issues involving his care;

(e) have her wishes and feelings taken into account, ss 22(4), 61 and 64 of the Children Act and para 25 *Principles and Practice*;

(f) have his race, culture, religion and background taken into account in care proceedings, s 1 of the Children Act and para 4 *Principles and Practice*;

(g) consult a solicitor of her own if of sufficient age and understanding;

(h) develop a sense of identity, para 19 *Principles and Practice*;

(i) grow to independence, para 26 *Principles and Practice*;

(j) to live in peace and safety, free from abuse, para 3 *Principles and Practice*.

7.6.6 Rights of parents of a child in care

Parents (with parental responsibility or not) and those with parental responsibility for a child in care, have the right to:

(a) consultation when plans are being made, para 2.53 *Residential Care*, paras 7 and para 10 *Principles and Practice*;

(b) information on where their child is being kept, Sched 2, para 15(2) Children Act;

(c) reasonable contact with their child s 34 Children Act, paras 14–16, *Principles and Practice*;

(d) receive financial or practical assistance with travelling to see their child Sched 2, para 16;

(e) be a party to written agreements about the child's placement *Residential Care*, para 2.63;

(f) participate actively in planning for the child's future, *Residential Care*, para 2.49.

Paragraph 2.49 of *Residential Care* states: 'The child's family, parents, grandparents, and other relatives involved with the child should be invited to participate actively in planning and to make their views known.'

7.7   Split hearings

Often, in cases of physical or sexual abuse, the case presents issues of fact which require determination, for example, the identity of an alleged abuser, dates, locations and circumstantial evidence, facts of alleged abuse etc. In care proceedings, to save the valuable time of court and experts, it may be appropriate to hold a two stage process (split hearing) in the court proceedings, see the guidance of Bracewell J in *Re S (Care Proceedings: Split Hearing)* [1996] 2 FLR 773.

In split hearings, the primary task of the court is to consider specific findings of fact, which will then assist the court in determining whether the applicant's evidence will meet the s 31 criteria, and therefore whether the grounds for a care or supervision order can be established. Once those facts are determined, the court can go on to the substantive hearing of the care proceedings.

Note that in the case of *Re B (Split Hearing: Jurisdiction)* [2000] 1 FLR 334, it was held that there is jurisdiction to hear an appeal on preliminary issues at a split hearing, if the findings of fact are crucial to the final decision.

7.8   Assessments and care planning

Only when the grounds (s 31 criteria) are established, will the court go on to consider what, if any order to make. The second task for the court, therefore, is to consider the circumstances of the child in the context of the underlying principles of the Children Act, and of the welfare checklist, and to decide whether the making of an order is necessary in the best interests of the child and, if so, which order would be the most appropriate in all the circumstances of the case. In order to assist the court, the applicant is expected to have provided a chronology, appropriate evidence and, also, a detailed care plan in which the proposed arrangements for the child are set out for the consideration of the court. See Chapter 16 below for discussion of the new publications *Framework for the Assessment of Children in Need and their Families* and *Assessing Children in Need and their Families*, Circular LAC 1999/29 and more information on care planning.

If the grounds are satisfied, much of the court's time will then be spent on assessment and discussion of the care plan, in order to assist the court to make the best decision for the child's short and long term future.

7.9   Effects of supervision order

A Supervision order places the child under the supervision of a local authority or a probation officer. The duties and powers of the supervising officer are set out in s 35 and Sched 3 to the Children Act, including a duty 'to advise, assist and befriend' the child. The supervising officer does not acquire parental responsibility for the child. The sanction for failure to co-operate with supervision is an application to discharge the order and to substitute something else, possibly a care order, see 8.9.3 below.

Directions may be made within supervision orders binding those responsible for the child and also the child to attend activities or live at specified places (see below, 7.9.3). They subsist for the duration of the supervision order or such lesser period as the court may specify.

A supervision order is possible within criminal proceedings on a finding of guilt against a juvenile offender, under s 7(7) of the Children and Young Persons Act 1969. Those orders may contain a direction that a child lives in local authority accommodation for a period of up to six months, but note that the criteria in s 31 do not have to be met before a 'criminal supervision order' is made, and also that a criminal court cannot make a care order. Criminal supervision orders are not discussed in this book, because they are different from orders made under s 31 of the Children Act. However, a child in local authority accommodation under a criminal supervision order must have the same rights under Vol 4 of the *Guidance*, *Residential Care*, as a child living away from home under a Children Act care or supervision order.

7.9.1 Interim orders

If a care or supervision application is adjourned, the court can make an interim order, s 38(1) of the Children Act. In the context of interim care or supervision orders, the court can make directions for medical or psychiatric assessment which a child of sufficient age and understanding may refuse, s 38(6) and (7); and the court may also make an exclusion requirement under s 38(A), ordering a named person to leave and/or excluding them from entering a dwelling house or defined geographical area in which the child lives. A power of arrest may be attached to the exclusion order, enforceable by the police, s 38(A)(5)–(9).

Where the court has power to impose an exclusion requirement in an interim care order, undertakings may be accepted from the relevant person, s 38(B). However, undertakings, although they are enforceable as an order of the court, cannot be coupled with a power of arrest.

Section 38(3) provides that if there is an application for care, but the court decides to make a residence order (for limited duration) instead of a care order, then the court must also make an interim supervision order unless it is satisfied that the child's welfare will be adequately safeguarded without one.

7.9.2 Duration of care and supervision

A supervision order may last for up to one year, s 91(3) and Sched 3, para 6 of the Children Act. It may be for shorter duration if so ordered by the court. A supervision order may also be extended for a further period or periods of up to a year, to a maximum of three years from the date it was first made, Sched 3, para 6(3) and (4) of the Children Act. Section 1 of the Children Act 1989 principles apply (see Chapter 2 above).

7.9.3 Directions in supervision orders

Directions to the child

The court may embody in the order specific requirements with which the child is to comply; and/or a general term along the lines that 'the child must comply with the directions given from time to time by the supervisor'. The supervisor then has a certain amount of leeway about the directions given, provided they fall within the parameters set in Sched 3, para 2 of the Children Act.

These are:

(a) to live at a place or places specified;

(b) to present himself to a person or persons specified for a period or periods specified;

(d) to participate in specified activities on dates and at times specified.

Directions to a 'responsible person'

A responsible person is defined in Sched 3, para 1 of the Children Act as 'a person who has parental responsibility for the child, and any other person with whom the child is living'.

Under Sched 3, with the consent of the responsible person, the court can include in the order a number of requirements:

(a) to take reasonable steps to ensure the child complies with the directions of the supervisor under Sched 3, para 2 (that is, to live at a specified place, present himself to a person specified on a specific day and to participate in activities);

(b) to take all reasonable steps to ensure the supervised child complies with directions regarding medical and psychiatric examinations (Sched 3, paras 3–5);

(c) that he or she comply with direction of supervisor 'to attend at a place specified in the directions for the purpose of taking part in activities so specified'.

A supervision order may also direct the responsible person to keep the supervisor informed of change of address, and to allow the supervisor to visit the child where they are living.

The responsible person may be directed to ensure the child complies with the supervisor's programme, giving the order a better chance of success. The adult may be asked to attend a treatment centre, to benefit the family and enable the child to remain at home.

The county court has no jurisdiction to accept undertakings in care or supervision cases, *Re B (A Minor) (Supervision Order: Parental Undertaking)* [1996] 1 FLR 676.

The court has no jurisdiction to specify the activities in which the responsible person (with their consent) is to participate. This is for the supervisor to arrange. The supervisor can therefore direct a sex offender to have treatment *Re H (Minors) (Terms of Supervision Orders)* [1994] Fam Law 486.

The court may authorise medical or psychiatric examination, and also direct attendance by the child and/or carers for medical or psychiatric examination of the child, or, if necessary, in-patient or outpatient treatment, which a child of sufficient understanding has a right to refuse (see Chapter 12 below, and Sched 3, paras 4 and 5 of the Children Act). Although the supervisor has the power to direct attendance by the child for medical or psychiatric examination or assessment, only the court can authorise medical or psychological examination. Before making these directions, the court must know that satisfactory arrangements have been, or can be, made for the treatment proposed. This implies that the practitioners concerned have indicated that they agree to carry it out. If the child has sufficient understanding, their consent is also required.

If a health practitioner is unwilling to continue treatment of the child, or the directions need altering because of any of the following circumstances:

(a) the treatment should be extended beyond the period specified in the order;

(b) different treatment is required;

(c) the child is not susceptible to treatment; or

(d) no further treatment is required,

he must submit a written report to the supervisor, who will then have to put that report back to the court for revision of the directions, Sched 3, para 5(6)–(7) of the Children Act.

7.9.4 Enforcement

If there is a direction that the supervisor visits the child, and this is prevented, then the supervisor may bring the matter back to court for a warrant for a police officer to 'assist the supervisor to exercise these powers, using reasonable force if necessary', s 102(1) of the Children Act. Other conditions cannot specifically be enforced, but their breach can be justification for bringing the matter back before the court for an application to discharge the supervision order, to seek a care order, or for a different order to be made.

The Court of Appeal has held that if a local authority wants to substitute care for supervision, it needs a specific application for a care order and the s 31 threshold criteria must be proved in support of the care application, *Re A (Minor) (Supervision Extension)* [1995] 2 FCR 114, CA.

7.10 Removal of child from care

Local authorities have a duty to look after and maintain children subject to care orders while they are in force, s 33(1) of the Children Act. A parent, or anyone else, may not remove a child from the care of the local authority without leave of the court. Removal of a child without permission of the local authority or leave of the court, keeping a child away from local authority care, or inciting a child to run away or stay away, is a criminal offence of child abduction under s 49 of the Children Act.

Note that if children are accommodated on a voluntary basis by a local authority (under ss 20–24 of the Children Act), the situation is different in that they may be removed at any time by a person with parental responsibility for them. A local authority has no power to keep a child in voluntary accommodation where there is a person with parental responsibility ready and willing to look after the child.

7.11 Variation, discharge and appeals

Care orders cease when the child reaches the age of 18, or earlier by order of the court (s 91(2)).

Supervision orders cease when directed by the court or on effluxion of time (see 8.9.2 above).

7.11.1 Variation and discharge

Applicant

A care or supervision order may be varied or discharged on the application of:

(a) any person with parental responsibility for the child;

(b) the child (who does not need leave of the court);

(c) in the case of supervision, the supervisor;

(d) in the case of a care order, the local authority with the responsibility for the child.

The application needs to be on form C1. Leave, if required, is on form C2, with a draft application in form C1 attached. The court should be that which made the original order. Other courts may accept the application if made with good reason.

Once made, the application may only be withdrawn with leave of the court, see r 5(1) FPC(CA)R 1991 and r 4.5(1)FPR 1991.

If the court discharges a care order it can order supervision, without having to re-prove the s 31(2) criteria, ss 39(4) and (5) of the Children Act.

Following an unsuccessful application to discharge a care order, there is no further application without leave within six months, s 91(5) of the Children Act. Under s 91(14) the court can order no further applications without leave, but should use this power sparingly, see *Re G* [1996] 2 FCR 1.

Notice

Applications for discharge should be made on notice. The applicant should serve each person entitled to notice with form C6A, with the date and time of the hearing endorsed on it, at least seven days before first directions or hearing. See r 4(3) FPC(CA)R 1991 and FPR 1991 r 4.4(3). Those entitled to notice are the same as for the original application.

Respondents

Those who are entitled to be respondents should be served with a notice of the proceedings in form C6, together with a draft of the application on form C1, at least seven days before the first directions or hearing. See r 4(1)(b) FPC(CA)R 1991 and r 4.4(1)(b) FPR 1991.

Those entitled to be respondents are those who were entitled to be, or were, respondents in the original application.

7.11.2 Appeals

Appeals against decisions concerning care orders lie from the family proceedings court to the High Court, and from the county court and the High Court to the Court of Appeal, see Chapter 17 below.

On refusal to make a care order, or on discharge, the court has power to make a care order pending appeal, s 40(1) and (2) of the Children Act; or to declare that the order appealed shall not take effect pending appeal, s 40(3). If the court of first instance refuses to make a care order pending appeal, the appeal court may make an interim care under s 38 Children Act.

7.12 Effects of the Human Rights Act 1998 on care and supervision proceedings

Public authorities must comply with the Human Rights Act 1998 and the European Convention for the Protection of Human Rights and Fundamental Freedoms (ECHR). Any acts by public authorities incompatible with these may be challenged by complaint, appeal or judicial review.

Failure to act is a ground for complaint or challenge, see ss 6 and 7 of the Human Rights Act 1998.

Section 22(4) allows retrospective challenge of acts which occurred before the Human Rights Act came into force.

Article 8 of the ECHR gives the right to respect for family life, home and correspondence. It may affect the interpretation of current law on contact, family involvement in care plans and care of children, post–adoption contact and the rights of children and their parents in the context of residential care. Watch case law as it unfolds in these areas of child protection law, since it provides an additional potential ground for appeal against local authority and court decisions and to challenge failures to act by public authorities. Article 6 (right to a fair trial) may provide an opportunity to encourage the involvement of children and families in decision making within care planning.

8 Secure Accommodation

Local authorities have a duty to provide accommodation for children in need in circumstances specified in s 20 of the Children Act 1989 (the 'Children Act') and may otherwise provide accommodation to safeguard or promote the welfare of a child. Secure accommodation is defined in s 25(1) of the Children Act as 'accommodation provided for the purpose of restricting liberty'.

Currently, the law relating to secure accommodation is complex, and in need of clarification. Children aged between 13 and 18 can be placed in secure accommodation for a variety of reasons. They may have committed a criminal offence and need to have their liberty restricted for their own safety or that of others. Orders made in these circumstances are called 'secure orders', to distinguish them from orders made in civil cases.

A child who is looked after by a local authority, or subject to a care order, may be kept in secure accommodation by the power given by a court order under s 25 of the Children Act. In certain circumstances, a child may be kept in secure accommodation by the consent of parents or those with parental responsibility.

Secure accommodation is currently governed by s 25 of the Children Act, by the Children (Secure Accommodation) Regulations 1991 SI 1991/1505 (the 'Secure Accommodation Regulations'); the Children (Secure Accommodation) (No 2) Regulations 1991 SI 1991/2034 and by the *Children Act 1989 Regulations and Guidance* Vol 4 *Residential Care* ('*Residential Care*'), Chapter 8, pp 118–29. It is also mentioned in *Children Act 1989 Regulations and Guidance* Vol 1 *Court Orders* ('*Court Orders*') at para 5.1.

A child below the age of 13 years may not be kept in secure accommodation without authority of the Secretary of State, reg 13(4), Secure Accommodation Regulations.

8.1   Effects of order

The effect of a secure accommodation order is restrict a child's liberty. Local authorities should pay careful regard to the guidance in their use of restriction of liberty. There is a distinction between placing a child in an environment (secure unit), from which he cannot run away and in which he is safeguarded; and the temporary restriction of a child's liberty, for example locking him in a room. There is a type of restraint, colloquially called 'pindown', formerly used in residential care, in which children who are disruptive or disobedient are punished by isolation in locked rooms, possibly with the additional deprivation of stimuli (for example, removal of their radios, TVs, writing and reading materials, sometimes even clothes), for periods varying from hours to days. Some residential children's homes even had specially adapted rooms set aside for this purpose. This type of punishment probably developed from a more moderate form of behavioural training called 'time out' to quieten overactive or disruptive children. 'Pindown' is a very severe form of 'time out', and has been much criticised in recent years because of the potentially emotionally abusive effect it can have on the child concerned. *Residential Care* at para 8.10 emphasises that 'any practice or measure which prevents a child from leaving a room or building of his own free will may be deemed by the court to be a restriction of liberty'. In the community homes system, the liberty of children may only be restricted in secure accommodation approved by the Secretary of State. There are other secure units outside the community homes system, for example, Youth Treatment Centres, which are covered by s 25.

In *Residential Care* at para 8.14 is clearly stated that:

> ... subject to the exclusions mentioned in para 8.13 [Children detained under the Mental Health Act 1983] ... no child, other than one looked after by a local authority who is accommodated in the circumstances defined, may have his liberty restricted unless the statutory criteria for the use of secure accommodation in s 25(1) of the Children Act applies. This applies equally to any proposed short term placement of the child in a locked room for 'time out' or seclusion purposes. The maximum period such a child may be kept in secure accommodation without the authority of the court is 72 hours, whether consecutively or in aggregate in any period of 28 days.

So, we have to conclude that 'time out' as a behavioural approach to child care is still contemplated, but is now subject to stricter regulation.

Safeguards

(a) Restriction of liberty should constitute a last resort, para 5(1) of *Court Orders*.

(b) Secure placements should be only for so long as necessary.

(c) Regular inspection and review by:
- Secretary of State (to approve secure unit);
- Social Services Inspectorate (general running and facilities);
- Department of Education (educational facilities);
- Regional Placements Committee (placements);
- Secure Accommodation Review Committee (resources).

(d) Time limits on the duration of secure accommodation orders.

(e) Care plans required by court on review of the orders.

(f) Each child has the right to an independent visitor.

(g) The 'three wise men (or women)'.

The local authority keeping a child in a secure unit must appoint at least three people, one of whom must not be a local authority employee, to review the placement within one month, and thereafter at three-monthly intervals. The task of these three is to ensure that the criteria justifying secure accommodation still applies, and that the placement is necessary, and no other description of accommodation is appropriate. See reg 15, Secure Accommodation Regulations. The local authority must keep good case records, with details listed in reg 17. The safeguards in s 25 also cover children accommodated by the National Health Service Trusts and local education authorities.

8.1.1 Criminal cases

In criminal proceedings, a child may be remanded or bailed to local authority accommodation under s 23 of the Children and Young Persons Act 1969. Once there, the child may behave in such a way that there is concern that the child may abscond, or injure himself or others. If this concern is justified, then the local authority or other named persons (see 8.4 below) may seek a secure order. The complication in the law at the moment is that the routes to the order and the rules applicable vary according to the court to which the child has been remanded. The grounds for the application in each of these circumstances are set out in 8.3 below, and procedures at 8.4. There is an excellent explanatory chart in 'Children Law and Practice' by Hershman, D and McFarlane, A, *Family Law*, Vol 1, p 396.

Juveniles may be detained by the police under circumstances specified in s 38 of the Police and Criminal Evidence Act 1984 ('PACE') and under s 38(6), the juvenile shall be moved to local authority accommodation unless the custody officer certifies that either it is impracticable to do so, or in the case of a juvenile over 12 years old, no secure accommodation is available and other local authority accommodation would not be adequate to protect the public from serious harm from him. Remands of juveniles to local authority accommodation by the police in this way are covered by the provisions of s 25 of the Children Act. There are also safeguards for young people arrested, protecting their interests in detention and during questioning. For discussion of PACE and its implications in practice, see Michael Zander's book, *Police and Criminal Evidence Act 1984* (3rd edn, 1995, London: Sweet & Maxwell).

Under s 130 of the Criminal Justice Act 1988, if juvenile offenders are remanded to local authority accommodation, and placed in secure units, their time so spent will be deducted from their eventual custodial sentence. See also Local Authority Circular LAC (88) 23, which reminds local authorities to keep accurate records of the duration of detention of children in secure units for the sentencing court.

8.1.2 Use of secure accommodation in civil cases

Paragraph 8.6 of *Residential Care* emphasises the local authority duty to 'take reasonable steps to avoid the need for children within their area to be placed in secure accommodation'. This duty is in Sched 2, para 7(c) Children Act, but also to 'encourage children within their area not to commit criminal offences', para 7(b). Placement decisions should be taken at a senior level, not lower than Assistant Director, accountable to the Director of Social Services. The placement should be part of the authority's overall plan for the child, and to safeguard and promote the child's welfare, s 22 of the Children Act.

8.2   Duration of secure accommodation

Without the authority of the court, a child may only have his liberty restricted for up to 72 hours, either consecutively or in aggregate within any period of 28 consecutive days, reg 10(1) Secure Accommodation Regulations.

Regulation 10(2) gives an exception where, if the court authorises secure accommodation for less than 28 days, on the day when the court order expires, the 28 day period mentioned in reg 10(1) starts running afresh from that day, ignoring any time spent in secure accommodation before the court order. Reg 10(3) gives special provisions for days either side of public holidays by granting a limited extension of the 72 hour time limit.

Where a child has been placed in local authority accommodation on a voluntary basis under s 20(1) of the Children Act, a person with parental responsibility can remove the child at any time, s 20(8), unless the exceptions in s 20(9) apply. This includes removal from secure accommodation.

8.2.1 Duration of court orders

Where the child has been remanded by a criminal court, the duration is for the period of the remand, with a maximum order of 28 days, reg 13 Secure Accommodation Regulations.

If the child is not on remand, or committed to the Crown Court, then the period is up to three months on the first application, reg 11, and up to six months on subsequent applications, reg 12.

In the case of *In Re W (A Minor) (Secure Accommodation Order)* [1993] 1 FLR 692 it was held that the court should consider the shortest appropriate period, rather than order the maximum period available as a matter of course.

The maximum period is three months on first order, and any period in the secure unit before the order is made should be deducted from this. *C (Minor) v Humberside CC and Another* [1995] 1 FCR 110. The justices making a care order had no power to order that a child kept in secure accommodation for a month should then be kept in the secure unit for a further three months.

The period of detention runs from the date the order was made, not the date the child was actually placed in the unit, see *Re B (Minor) (Secure Accommodation)* [1994] 2 FLR 707.

If the criteria for detention in secure accommodation cease to apply, the child must be released, *LM v Essex CC* [1999] 1 FLR 988.

8.2.2 Adjournments

If there is an adjournment of an application for secure accommodation, then, under s 25(5) of the Children Act, the court may permit the child to be kept secure during the adjournment. There is here an obvious risk of getting the order sought by the back door, perhaps without adequate proof of its necessity, particularly if the adjournment is for further evidence to become available. The court has provided a safeguard in stating that the adjournment may not be longer than the maximum periods for the order under regs 11 and 12, see *C v Humberside CC and Another* [1994] 2 FLR 759.

8.3   Grounds for application

Section 25 of the Children Act provides that if:

(a) (i) the child has a history of absconding and is likely to abscond from any other description of accommodation; and

(ii) if he absconds he is likely to suffer significant harm; or

(b) that if he is kept in any other description of accommodation, he is likely to injure himself or others,

he can be placed in local authority accommodation by the court under s 23 of the Children and Young Persons Act 1969.

This provision applies to children who are:

(a) charged with or convicted of an offence which would carry a sentence of 14 years or more for a person over 21 years old;

(b) charged with or convicted of an offence of violence, or who have a previous conviction for violence;

(c) detained under s 38(6) of PACE 1984.

The criteria for those placed under s 23 of the Children and Young Persons Act 1969 are differently worded from the criteria for those placed under reg 6(2) Secure Accommodation Regulations. This regulation provides that a child may not be kept in secure accommodation unless it appears that any accommodation other than that provided for the purpose of restricting his liberty is inappropriate because:

(a) the child is likely to abscond from such accommodation;

(b) the child is likely to injure himself or other people if he is kept in any such accommodation.

Note that the likelihood of significant harm is omitted in this regulation. In the case *of Re M (A Minor) (Secure Accommodation Order)* [1995] 2 FCR 373 the welfare of the child was held by the court to be relevant, but not paramount in s 25 proceedings, and therefore application of the welfare checklist, although useful, was not obligatory.

A child may be placed in a secure unit under s 25(1) to prevent her injuring another child, which may be inconsistent with putting the welfare of the secured child first. The court's duty mirrors that of the local authority under s 20(1)(b) of the Children Act. The court must ascertain whether the s 25 conditions are satisfied, and if so, to make the order if this accords with the duty of the local authority to safeguard and promote the welfare of the child. The guardian ad litem will assist the court in deciding these questions: *Re M (Secure Accommodation Order)* [1995] Fam 108; [1995] 3 All ER 407; [1995] 1 FLR 418.

8.4   Practice and procedure

Secure accommodation orders are not included in the definition of 'family proceedings' in s 8 of the Children Act, but because s 92(2) says that 'all proceedings under the Act shall be treated as family proceedings in relation to magistrates' courts', this means that in the Family Proceedings Court, s 25 applications are included. The 'menu' of orders available in family proceedings is therefore open to the court, including s 8 orders and others which the court can make of its own volition (see Figure 8, below, pp 124–25).

8.4.1 Application

Where a child is being looked after by a local authority (even if the child is accommodated by another body) that local authority should be the applicant for the order. In other circumstances, other potential applicants include those who are providing accommodation for the child, that is:

(a) local authority;

(b) health authority or NHS Trust;

(c) local education authority;

(d) person carrying on residential home, nursing home, or mental nursing home.

Once made, an application may only be withdrawn with leave of the court.

8.4.2 Forms

The application should be made on form C1 together with form C20 in accordance with Sched 1 to the Family Proceedings Courts (Children Act) Rules 1991 (FPC(CA)R), and App 1 Family Proceedings Rules 1991 (FPR).

If the application is made to the High Court in wardship, it should be by summons and the ward should be named as a party, r 5(5) FPR 1991 as amended by the Family Proceedings (Amendment) Rules 1992 SI 1992/456.

8.4.3 Venue

Secure accommodation orders can be made at any level of the court. They can be made in criminal proceedings at the youth court or at a higher level of criminal court; and in the Family Proceedings Court or the county court or High Court in the course of other proceedings.

8.4.4 Respondents

Respondents should be served with a copy of the application in form C1 with C20, with the date of hearing or directions, and notice of the proceedings with the date and place of hearing, FPC(CA)R, r 4(1)(b), and r 4.4(1)(b) FPR 1991.

Service should be one day before the hearing; r 4(4) FPC(CA)R and r 4.4(4) FPR 1991.

Certain people are automatically respondents to the application:

(a) those believed to have parental responsibility for the child;

(b) those who had parental responsibility prior to the care order, if one is in force;

(c) the child.

Others may be joined as respondents, and automatic respondents may be removed by direction of the court. See r 7(1) FPC(CA)R and r 4.7(1) FPR 1991.

If the application is made to the High Court in wardship, the ward should be named as a party, r 5(5) FPR as amended by the Family Proceedings (Amendment) Rules 1992 SI 1992/456.

8.4.5 Notice

Applications for secure accommodation must be made on one day's notice, r 4(4) FPC(CA)R, and r 4.4(4) FPR 1991.

The following people are entitled to notice of the proceedings, with the date, time and place of the hearing:

(a) a local authority providing accommodation for the child;

(b) any person with whom the child was living at the time proceedings were commenced;

(c) person providing a refuge for the child under s 51 of the Children Act.

Schedule 2 col (iv) FPC(CA)R and App 3 col (iii) FPR 1991.

Rule 4(3) FPC(CA)R, and r 4.4(3) FPR 1991 provide that if a child is placed in a secure unit in a community home, and there is an application to keep the child there, certain people need to be informed as soon as practicable:

(a) the child's parents;

(b) any person with parental responsibility for the child;

(c) the child's independent visitor;

(d) any other person the local authority considers should be told.

8.4.6 Service

Service is effected on a solicitor for a party by delivery at his office, by first class post at the office or through the DX, or by fax to the office.

Service on a party who has no solicitor is by delivery to that party personally, or by delivery of first class post to his address, r 8 FPC(CA)R, and r 4.8 FPR 1991.

Service on a child may be through her solicitor, or the guardian ad litem, or, with leave of the court, service on the child herself, r 8 (4) FPC(CA)R, and r 4.8(4) FPR 1991.

The time for service may be abridged by the court, or waived altogether, see r 8(8) FPC(CA)R and r 4.8(8) FPR 1991.

8.5   Role of the guardian ad litem

These proceedings are 'specified proceedings' within the meaning of s 41 of the Children Act and therefore a guardian ad litem must be appointed by the court unless it is of the opinion that it is unnecessary to do so in order to safeguard the child's interests. This is a protective measure intended to ensure that children in secure units have had their wishes and feelings made known to the court, and that the court has been advised of the most appropriate way forward in the best interests of the child. Children who are accommodated on a voluntary basis under s 20(1) of the Children Act are also safeguarded by this provision. Note that from April 2001, the CAFCASS proposals will be implemented, changing the structure of Guardian Ad Litem Panels. Watch legal journals for details.

8.6   Contact

Children in secure units have the right to reasonable contact with members of their family, as children in care (see above, 7.6.4. and below, 12.5. Since a s 25 application in a magistrates' court amounts to 'family proceedings' under s 8 of the Children Act, provided there is no care order in force, it is possible for the court to make a s 8 contact order to run alongside the secure accommodation order. A s 8 contact order can also co-exist with a supervision order. If the child is in care, then a s 34 care contact order may be made if necessary.

8.7   Rights of the child

These are:

(a) three persons to review placement, reg 15, Secure Accommodation Regulations;

(b) duty on local authority to keep detailed case records, reg 17;

(c) education whilst accommodated;

(d) entitlement to appropriate therapy where necessary;

(e) regular inspection of the secure unit by the Social Services Inspectorate from the Department of Health, who must approve the unit;

(f) inspection by the Department of Education, because children there are receiving education whilst accommodated;

(g) regional placement committees, who check the resources and conditions of the unit;

(g) time limits on the duration of secure accommodation orders;

(i) care plans on review of the orders;

(j) independent visitor;

(k) consultation, and to have wishes and feelings ascertained, s 22(4) of the Children Act;

(k) consultation with parents and those with parental responsibility, s 22(4) of the Children Act; and

(l) 'free' legal aid to be represented on s 25 application.

8.7.1 Legal aid

Section 99 of the Children Act amends the Legal Aid Act 1988 ensuring legal aid is granted to a child subject to a s 25 Children Act application, who wishes to be legally represented. Legal aid is 'free', that is, non-means and non-merits tested, available on completion of form CLA5A by the solicitor. The court may not make a secure accommodation order on an unrepresented child. The only exception is where the child has been informed of her right to apply for legal aid, and having been given the opportunity to do so, has failed to apply or refused to do so, s 25(6) Children Act.

8.8   Appeals and the Human Rights Act 1998

Section 94 of the Children Act makes provision for appeals to the High Court against decisions or refusals to authorise applications for the restriction of liberty. The placement in secure accommodation may continue whilst an appeal against authorisation is waiting to be determined. If the appeal is against a refusal to authorise the child may not be detained in a secure unit pending appeal. Appeals from the county court or High Court lie to the Court of Appeal.

The Human Rights Act 1998 and Art 5 of the European Convention for the Protection of Human Rights and Fundamental Freedoms (ECHR) is relevant to decisions of local authorities and the courts in secure accommodation issues. Article 5 confirms the right to liberty and security of a person and Art 8 protects the right to family life. Art 5 refers to the detention of minors for 'educational supervision' or for the purpose of 'bringing them before the competent legal authority'.

Acts of public authorities and the courts which do not comply with the Human Rights Act or the ECHR may be challenged by complaint, judicial review, or appeal. Note that past acts may also be challenged, s 22(4).

9 Education Supervision Orders

Education between five and 16 years is compulsory. The Education Act 1996 (the 'Education Act') combined with the provisions of s 36 and Sched 3 to the Children Act 1989 (the 'Children Act'), authorises prosecution of parents who fail to ensure that their child receives a proper full time education. Parents have the right to educate their children other than in school, provided that the child receives a 'proper education' as described below. The local education authority may agree, under the Education Act 1996, to help parents to arrange education otherwise than at school.

The Children Act in s 36(4) states that 'a child is being properly educated only if he is receiving efficient full time education suitable to his age, ability and aptitude, and any special educational needs he may have'. Under s 437 of the Education Act, a local education authority which is concerned about a child's education, may serve notice on parents to show that the child is being properly educated. If the parents fail to comply or to provide the required proof, then the the local education authority may serve on parents a 'school attendance order', requiring the parents to register the child at a named school. Failure to comply with this order constitutes an offence, and on prosecution, the court may direct the local education authority to apply for an education supervision order.

9.1 Effects of an education supervision order

An education supervision order, made under s 36 of the Children Act places the child under the supervision of a local education authority. These differ from supervision orders made under s 31. School refusal is no longer by itself a ground for care, but it may be evidence of neglect, lack of parental control, underlying emotional problems, or that the education system may be failing to meet the needs of the child. School refusal may, therefore, form part of the s 31 grounds, see Chapter 7 above, and *Re O (A Minor) (Care Order: Education Procedure)* [1992] 2 FLR 7.

The Children Act, in para 12 of Sched 3 sets out the supervisor's duty to 'advise, assist and befriend and give directions to the supervised child and to his parents', 'in such as way as will ... secure that he is properly educated'.

The supervisor should take into account the wishes and feelings of the child and parents, and directions made should be reasonable, and such that the parents and child are able to comply with them. Persistent failure to comply with directions may lead to prosecution.

Paragraph 18 of Sched 3 to the Children Act sets out the defences to a prosecution for failure to comply with a school attendance order, which includes: showing that all reasonable steps were taken to comply; or that the the directions were unreasonable; or that there was compliance with directions or requirements in a supervision order and that it was not reasonably practicable to comply with both the supervision order and the school attendance order.

Children Act 1989 Regulations and Guidance Vol 7 *Guardians ad Litem and Other Court-Related Issues* ('*Guardians ad Litem*') discusses directions in paras 3.31–3.35. Directions might require the child to attend meetings with the supervisor or with teachers at the school to discuss progress, or cover medical assessment or examination, or assessment by a clinical psychologist. They should be confirmed in writing, and the parents informed.

Under Sched 3 para 13 of the Children Act, parents lose their right to have the child educated at home, or move the child to another school, while an education supervision order is in force, and they have no right of appeal against admissions decisions.

Volume 7 of the Guidance, *Guardians ad Litem*, is made under s 7 of the Local Authority Social Services Act 1970, and so local authorities must follow it unless there are cogent local reasons not to comply. Non-compliance with chapter 3 is *prima facie* ground for complaint, and will have to be justified if challenged. However, note *Essex CC v B* [1993] 1 FLR 866.

9.2   Duration

The order will subsist for one year, or until the child is no longer of compulsory school age, whichever is the earlier, para 15(1) and (6),

Sched 3 to the Children Act. It may be discharged earlier, on the application of the child, the parents, or the local education authority, para 17(1), Sched 3 to the Children Act.

It may be extended for up to three years if application is made within three months before the expiry date, and it can be extended more than once, para 15, Sched 3. It will cease on the making of a care order, Sched 3, para 15(6)(b).

9.3   Grounds for application

Under s 36(3) of the Children Act, an order may only be made if the court is 'satisfied that the child concerned is of compulsory school age and is not being properly educated'; s 36(4) states that 'a child is being properly educated only if he is receiving efficient full time education suitable to his age, ability and aptitude, and any special educational needs he may have'.

Where a child is the subject to a school attendance order under s 437 of the Education Act which is in force but with which the child is not complying, or is a registered pupil of a school which he is not attending regularly within the meaning of s 444 of the Education Act; there is a presumption that the child is not being properly educated, see s 36(5) of the Children Act.

Note that an order may not be sought in respect of a child who is already subject to a care order, s 36(6) of the Children Act.

Before making an application for an education supervision order, the local education authority are required under s 36(8) of the Children Act to consult social services. *Guardians ad Litem* para 3(18) requires everyone to make all reasonable efforts to resolve a problem of poor school attendance without the use of legal sanctions: 'Many attendance difficulties can be overcome by sensitive action by schools and the Education Welfare Service.' Paragraph 3.10 requires the outcome of the consultation to be confirmed in writing, indicating whether the social services department is involved with the child or the family, and if there are any known reasons why an education supervision order would not be appropriate. The social services department may seek the assistance of the education authority in the provision of services for the child, who are under a duty to comply with the request in accordance with s 27(1)–(3) of the Children Act. There is a reciprocal arrangement in s 27(4) which also requires every local authority to assist any local education authority with the provision of services for any child within the local authority's area who has special educational needs.

9.4   Practice and procedure

9.4.1 Application

The applicant is the local education authority. The application should be made on form C17. Applications to renew an order are made on form C17A. Applications are 'family proceedings' under s 8(3) and (4) of the Children Act, and therefore the menu of orders is available to the court (see Figure 8, below, pp 124–25). The principles in s 1 of the Children Act apply, see Chapter 2 above. An application may not be made in respect of a child subject to a care order, s 36(6) of the Children Act.

9.4.2 Venue

Cases should be commenced in the Family Proceedings Court, but may be transferred to the county court or the High Court. If the county court or the High Court has directed an investigation of the child's circumstances under s 37(1) of the Children Act, the application may be made to that court or a nominated care centre. If there are proceedings pending in a court, then the application may commence there.

9.4.3 Notice

Rule 9(3)(4) Family Proceedings Court (Children Act) 1989 Rules 1991 SI 1991/1395 and r 4.9(3)(4) Family Proceedings Rules 1991 SI 1991/1247 provide that seven days' notice of the hearing or directions appointment must be given, with the date and venue of the application.

A local authority providing accommodation for the child, or the person with whom a child is living, or the manager of a refuge providing accommodation for the child under s 51 of the Children Act may be served with notice of the application, r 4 Family Proceedings Court (Children Act) Rules and r 4.4 Family Proceedings Rules 1991.

9.4.4 Respondents

Every person with parental responsibility for the child is a respondent, as is the child. Respondents should be served with notice of the application, together with a copy of the application in form C17. Respondents may file and serve an answer two days before the hearing.

9.4.5 Service

The normal rules of service apply, see r 4 Family Proceedings Court (Children Act) Rules and r 4.4 Family Proceedings Rules 1991. The court also has power under the rules to vary or waive service.

9.5 Rights of the child

These are:

(a) the child's welfare is paramount;

(b) to be consulted on schooling issues;

(c) to have wishes and feelings taken into consideration;

(d) to be a respondent in the application if of sufficient age and understanding;

(e) to receive directions that are reasonable;

(f) to advice, assistance and befriending from the supervisor.

9.6 Variation, discharge and appeals

Discharge can be on the application of the child, the parents, or the local education authority, para 17(1), Sched 3 to the Children Act. The court on discharge may order the local authority to investigate the child's circumstances under s 37 and para 17(2), Sched 3 to the Children Act.

The order may be extended for up to three years on application by the authority within three months before the expiry date, and the order can be extended more than once, para 15, Sched 3 of the Children Act.

Appeals

Appeal from the magistrates lies with the High Court, s of the 49 Children Act. Orders made in the county court or High Court may be appealed to the Court of Appeal.

Interestingly, the European Convention for the Protection of Human Rights envisages the use of secure accommodation to detain a minor for 'educational supervision', Art 5.

However, read in conjunction with Art 8 (right to family life), it is unlikely that in the UK this would encourage courts to take a step in that direction, but it would be interesting to watch case law as it develops in this area.

10 Police Powers Under the Children Act 1989

Police have special powers under s 46 of the Children Act 1989 (the 'Children Act') referred to as 'police protection', which do not need a court order. The ground for action is that police have reasonable cause to believe the child would otherwise suffer significant harm, s 46(2).

These powers are:

(a) to remove a child to a safe place and keep him there, s 46(1)(a);

(b) to prevent a child's removal from a safe place, s 46(1)(b);

(c) no power to enter premises without a warrant unless s 17 Police and Criminal Evidence Act 1984 satisfied (s 17 includes saving life and limb, prevention of serious damage to property, or arrests);

(d) police must safeguard and promote the child's welfare, s 46(9)(b).

The maximum duration for the exercise of s 46 powers is 72 hours, s 46(6).

Each area must have a 'designated police officer' responsible for carrying out the duties imposed by the Children Act, who can apply for emergency protection if necessary, ss 46(3)(e) and 46(7).

The police must, under s 46(3), inform the local authority of their action, the reasons for it, and the child's whereabouts; inform the child and discover his wishes and feelings; remove the child to local authority accommodation and, under s 46(4), take reasonable steps to inform parents, those with parental responsibility, and those with whom the child was living, of the action, the reasons for it, and future plans.

11 Taking Instructions in Family Proceedings

Family proceedings are non adversarial. Advocates may be instructed to represent children, parents, other parties, or local authorities; and effective advocacy depends more on thorough preparation of the case, coupled with good negotiation skills with all parties throughout the proceedings than on the final presentation in court.

The first task is to elicit from all sources available as much information as possible about the circumstances of the case, the client, and the child. All evidence relevant to the welfare of the child should be available to the court.

11.1 Action plan on receipt of instructions from adult or local authority

(Taking instructions from child clients is discussed below, 15.3.)

(a) Arrange to interview the client or instructing social worker as soon as possible.

(b) Where appropriate, check the legal aid situation and complete the necessary forms (see below, 17.1).

(c) Obtain copies of applications and documents which have been filed with the court.

(d) Are there other relevant proceedings current or pending? Obtain details.

(e) Have there been previous proceedings in relation to the child(ren) or the family?

If so, ask for copies of court orders and copies of documents filed with the court.

(f) Check who are the other parties in the case.

(g) Ascertain whether other parties have instructed advocates, and obtain details.

(h) Let the court and all other parties (or their advocates if they are represented) and the guardian ad litem know you are instructed in the matter, and write, inviting communication and offering co-operation.

(See Chapter 15 if you are instructed by the guardian ad litem on behalf of the child.)

(i) Interview potential witnesses.

11.2 Interviewing clients

Cases involving family breakup or issues of child protection are stressful for all the parties concerned. It is essential to establish a relationship of trust with clients, giving them space in the initial interview to express their feelings, whilst at the same time keeping the interview focused on taking background history and instructions. Set aside sufficient time to allow clients to fully express all they have to say and offer appropriate refreshments – this can provide a welcome break. A checklist may assist to keep the interview focused on the information required. Below are sample checklists of some basic issues to cover when interviewing parents, social workers, and medical witnesses, to which can be added specific issues relevant to each specific case.

Checklist for information from parents

Full name

Address

Home telephone number
(Any problems/restrictions on its use?)

Work telephone number
(Any problems/restrictions on its use?)

Mobile telephone number
(Any problems/restrictions on its use?)

Names of all the children of the family and their dates of birth.

Who are the parents of each child of the family?

Where does each child of the family live, if they do not live with the client?

What are the contact arrangements with the children living elsewhere?

Partner and family members living in client's household

Close or significant family members living outside household

The family's social/cultural/racial/ religious context

Does this client, any member of the family, or the child(ren), have any special needs, cultural issues, language problems, etc of which the court, guardian ad litem and parties need to be aware?

General information about this client, including: background, education, attainments, current or past employment, interests, and significant life events

Does this client, or any partner, family member, carer, or co-habitee, have any convictions for offences which may affect an assessment of their capacity to care for the child(ren)? For example, conviction for an offence listed in Sched 1 of the Children and Young Persons Act 1933, drink or drugs related offences, etc?

Convictions should be disclosed to the court: *Re R (Minors) (Custody)* [1986] 1 FLR 6

Does the client or any family member have any particular skills or attributes relevant to their parenting ability?

Have there been any court orders or applications made to a court in respect of a child of the family or any family member?

Other people involved with the family who may be able to assist in providing information:

(a) schools attended by the child(ren)

(b) playgroups

(c) voluntary organisations/religious organisations

(d) therapists

(e) GP/hospital

(f) health visitor

How does the client see the present situation; what were the circumstances that led up to this application?

Does the client have any comments to make or explanations to offer about causation of any injuries or harm alleged, or the child's emotional problems?

What contact has the client had to date with social services, or other professionals about this child?

Has the client requested or received any help, advice, or resources from social services?

What would the client like to see happen in the future concerning the child(ren)?

What would the child(ren) like to happen?

What does the client think that others will say about the situation? (Often a very revealing question)

Can the client think of others who may be able to offer relevant information about the child or family?

Checklist for information from social workers

Full name

Office address

Office telephone number

Post held

Relevant qualifications

Relevant experience

Reason for involvement with the family, or initial referral to social services department (check confidentiality, for example does the location of the child require protection or is there sensitive information in this report?)

Date of initial involvement with child/family

Dates of subsequent involvement, in chronological order, including:

(a)   whom seen

(b)   venues

(c)   duration

(d)   documents referred to

(e)   other contacts, for example, by telephone

Description of the composition of immediate and wider family

Put the family in its social/cultural/racial context

Define any special needs, cultural requirements, language problems, etc

Education/background/attainments of parents/carers/siblings where relevant

Does any family member, carer, co-habitee, have any convictions? Details should be obtained and made available for the court

Does any family member have any particular skills/attributes relevant to parenting ability?

Are there any previous court orders or applications made to a court in respect of a child of the family or family member?

Chronology of all social work involvement and interventions with the family to date (including conferences, Child Protection Register, reviews planning meetings, etc)

Other professionals involved with the family:

(a) schools attended by the child(ren)

(b) playgroups

(c) voluntary and/or religious organisations

(d) therapists

(e) family aide

Medical history of the child:

(a) GP

(b) health visitor

(c) hospital admissions recorded

Observations ... personality, physical appearance and demeanour of the child and characteristics of carers/parents/wider family members where relevant

Outline the presenting problems within this family: home circumstances; assessment of family needs and assessment of the significant harm criteria in s 31 of the Children Act 1989, including:

(a)   the past harm to the child

(b)   current harm to the child

(c)   future risk of harm to the child

See recent guidance *Framework for Assessment of Need* ('*Framework for Assessment*') and *Assessing Children in Need and their Families* ('*Assessing Children in Need*') (both 2000, London: HMSO) and LAC 99/29. Has the local authority complied?

Attitudes of the parents/carers/child to presenting problems:

(a)   explanations offered as to causation of injuries

(b)   explanations offered as to causation of emotional problems

In relation to video-recorded interviews or children's disclosures, note *Memorandum of Good Practice in Video-Recorded Interviews*, 1992, London: HMSO and *Interviewing Child Witnesses Under the Memorandum of Good Practice*, 1999, Home Office. These give excellent guidance on procedure. Has the local authority complied?

When interviewing children, or others, social workers should carefully make a record of all questions and responses made, as soon as possible, in chronological order and have the original records available at court

In your view, can the parents/carers control the child?

(If not, how does the lack of control show and what are the apparent reasons?)

Attitude of family/child to the provision of services/protection measures

Options for consideration, see the list of court orders in the Sources list above, 1.3

What are the wishes and feelings of the family in relation to the options discussed with them?

What are the wishes and feelings of the child(ren) about the options discussed with them?

Which is the preferred option for social services point of view acting in the best interests of the child?

Care plan and written agreements (bearing in mind *The Children Act 1989 Guidance and Regulations* Vol 3 *Family Placements*, pp 15–16, para 2.62, also *Framework for Assessment* and *Assessing Children in Need* and LAC 99/29). See, also, above, 7.6 and below, Chapter 16

Other relevant considerations

Bear in mind the welfare checklist

Checklist for information from medical witnesses

Witness's full name

Health centre/surgery/hospital address

Post held

Relevant qualifications and experience

Ensure that any opinions expressed are objective, relevant, and supported by observations

Nature, extent, venue and duration of examination(s) of the child:

(a)   date, duration and venue of first examination

(b)   reason for referral

(c)   observations of child on examination

(d)   appearance, demeanour, attitude to examination and others present

(e)   note any statements made by the child or by others that are relevant

(f)   any abnormalities in physical or mental state

(g)   marks, abrasions, wounds, skeletal survey, pain, tenderness

(h)   unusual features or appearance of any part of the body

Body map showing location of areas of injury, bruising etc can be very helpful

Colour photographs are of great help to a court if the child/family is willing to allow this, but beware, if sexual abuse is alleged, photography may remind child of the abuse or be further abusive

Description of the general health of the child

Full description of the child's injuries/abnormalities, with an explanation of the medical terms used.

Is it possible to give a time of the occurrence of any injuries noted?

When the injuries occurred, would they have caused pain to the child? Would he or she have cried out, screamed in pain? Does it still hurt? How soon afterwards would it stop hurting? Should a caring adult have noticed/treated the child's discomfort/pain?

Were there attempts to treat the injuries/or to cover them up?

Is there any evidence of brittle bones or other congenital factor likely to contribute to these injuries or explain them?

If anyone was questioned about the injuries, note who was questioned, who was present, their reactions and demeanour in response to questioning, specific questions used, and responses given

Note any comments or explanations offered of how the injuries/abnormalities occurred

Does any explanation given by adults agree/conflict with the medical or psychiatric diagnosis?

Describe diagnosis, treatment given or recommended following examination and prognosis

Note date(s), venue and duration of subsequent examinations

Record any other relevant or significant health issues within family (including parents, siblings, other relatives), particularly any issues affecting the parents' or carers' ability to look after the child, or affecting the general health and welfare of the child or close family members

Health history of the child, in chronological order, including:

(a) physical development

(b) height/weight/centile charts

(c) developmental assessments according to age

(d) visual/hearing/neurological/speech/language assessments

(e) evidence of emotional problems/abnormalities (have they been diagnosed as a congenital disorder, or is there possibly some other cause?)

(f) evidence of physical problems/abnormalities. (Do they constitute an illness or 'disability' within the meaning of the Children Act? Have they been diagnosed as a congenital disorder, or is there possibly some other cause?)

(g) treatment(s) given to the child

(h) what was the effect of treatment?

(i) advice offered to the family/child about medical care

(j) was the advice taken up and acted upon?

Up to date information about the child's development

Other information concerning the child's welfare that is relevant for the helping agencies and the court

Witnesses should bear in mind the welfare checklist whilst writing their statement. It is a useful reference concerning the best interests of the child shared by the court, the guardian ad litem and the professionals in the case.

Include the names and addresses of doctors and other health professionals who have been involved with the child/family, or to whom child the child has been referred for specialist treatment or examination. They may be able to give additional relevant information.

Include a list of 'dates to avoid', that is, times when unavailable for court, conferences and meetings.

11.3 Preparation of the case

Good advocacy is not just an ability to speak persuasively in court. It is 90% good preparation. Effective advocates are non-adversarial in approach, willing to negotiate, and when in court, they are courteous, clear, concise and accurate, having read all the case documentation thoroughly before the hearing.

A sound knowledge of the relevant law and the rules of evidence and procedure is essential; but it is vitally important to keep up to date with changes. For essential and wider reference lists, see Chapter 19.

11.4 Burden of proof in child law cases

Generally, the person alleging a fact must prove it. In child protection, the burden of proof is on a balance of probability, that is 'it is more likely than not' that there is actual or a potential risk of significant harm to the child. In *Re H and Others (Minors) (Sexual Abuse: Standard of Proof)* [1996] 1 FLR 80 and [1996] 1 FCR 509 the House of Lords considered the standard of proof of sexual abuse, concluding 'the more serious the allegation, the less likely it is that the event occurred, and, hence, the stronger should be the evidence before the court concludes that the allegation is established on a balance of probability' (*per* Lord Nicholls of Birkenhead).

11.5 Special evidence rules in child law cases

Child law cases should be non-adversarial. The focus of the case is the welfare of the child. The rules of evidence in child protection differ from other areas of law. The Children Act encourages admission of actions affecting the child without these becoming the basis for prosecution. In wardship proceedings the strict rules of evidence do not apply, see Butler-Sloss LJ in *Re H (Minor), Re K (Minors) (Child abuse: Evidence)* [1989] 2 FLR 313, pp 332–33. The general rules of evidence in non-child law cases render certain evidence inadmissible, that is, that relating to character, hearsay, evidence obtained by illicit means (for example, covert video surveillance) and opinion. In child law cases these rules are different.

11.5.1   Character

In child law cases, consideration of the character of those who care for the child is vitally important and evidence which tends to show their characteristics is admitted.

11.5.2   Best evidence and hearsay

The hearsay rule provides that witnesses may only give an account of what they themselves actually experienced as evidence of the truth of the alleged event. If a witness tells the court what someone else said, the words quoted cannot be admitted as proof that the thing reported actually happened. If A tells the court that 'On 14 July 2000, B said, "C hit me"', under the hearsay rule, this statement proves only that on that day B was alive and able to speak; that B spoke to A and that A heard his words; but it is not sufficient to prove that C did in fact hit B. B personally would have to come and give evidence of the event.

In child law cases, however, the court requires all relevant evidence, and in certain circumstances, it admits hearsay. The wishes and feelings of children are important, and quotations from others about the child or of what the child said can be vital. Section 96(3) of the Children Act, and the Children (Admissibility of Hearsay Evidence) Order 1993 SI 1993/621 provide that in civil proceedings before the High Court or a county court, and family proceedings, and civil proceedings in a magistrates' court under the Child Support Act 1991, evidence given in connection with the upbringing, maintenance or welfare of a child, shall be admissible notwithstanding any rule of law relating to hearsay. Family proceedings are defined in ss 8(3) and 105 of the Children Act. Refer to s 4 of the Civil Evidence Act 1995 for helpful criteria in assessment of hearsay evidence.

The court requires the original of any notes produced, that is, those made contemporaneously, not neatly typed copies made later on. Notes should be written up at the time or as soon as possible after the event recorded. If notes are made days after an event their reliability may be questioned.

11.5.3 Opinion

Witnesses may give factual or expert evidence. Witnesses of fact may not give their opinion and are expected to restrict themselves to a full and accurate account of what happened. The court draws inferences from the facts. Experts may draw inferences, and offer opinions based on the facts, research and their own learning and experience. They should behave in a professional manner, and be impartial, see Chapter18.

11.5.4 Statements made by guardians ad litem

Under s 41(11)(a)–(b) of the Children Act, the court may take account of any statement contained in the report of a guardian ad litem, and of any evidence given in respect of matters referred to in the guardian's report. The court has the power to regulate its own proceedings, and will assess the weight to give to such evidence. The guardian ad litem has access to and may cite local authority records, see s 42 of the Children Act; and should draw to the attention of the court for directions any local authority papers which are relevant, but which the local authority does not intend to disclose, see *Re C (Expert Evidence:Disclosure: Practice)* [1995] 1 FLR 204.

11.5.5   No professional privilege for medical or psychiatric reports

Medical records must be disclosed on production of a subpoena *duces tecum* issued with leave of a District Judge. *Practice Direction (Family Proceedings: Case Management)* [1995] 1 FLR 456 requires full and frank disclosure of material in all matters relating to children, because the welfare of the child is of paramount importance. This includes medical reports unfavourable to a client's interests, see *Essex CC v R (A Minor)* [1993] 2 FLR 826, and *Oxfordshire CC v M* [1994] 1 FLR 175, in which the Court of Appeal upheld this principle. Communications between lawyer and client remain privileged.

11.5.6   Directions hearings – ordering the evidence

Delay must be avoided, s 1(3) of the Children Act. Directions appointments enable the court to control the preparation of evidence and listing hearings. The Children Act Advisory Committee has produced a useful pro forma for standard directions for both public and private family law proceedings.

Leave of the court is required for disclosure of documents to experts or to other non parties; to withhold evidence from a party; and for medical or psychiatric examinations or assessments of children. Where one party seeks to prevent another from seeing a document, an application should be made on notice and transferred to the High Court (*Re M (Disclosure)* [1998] 2 FLR 1028). The directions may also stipulate the venue of any assessments to be carried out, who should accompany the child and to whom the results should be given.

Most of us use expert witnesses on a fairly regular basis, developing good working relationships. See chapter 18 for instruction of experts, judicial guidance, how to find the right expert and resource issues. Before the directions hearing the advocate should ascertain whether selected experts are available, how long assessments will take, cost, legal aid and any assistance the experts may require. The expert should confirm availability, enabling the court to fix a suitable hearing date.

11.6 Court procedure at the hearing

Procedure is addressed separately in the chapters dealing with each order. However, hearings follow a reasonably consistent pattern common to most Children Act applications.

Figure 6: Admissible evidence in care proceedings

ORAL EVIDENCE may be given by:

The child themselves ...	Provided that the court is satisfied on enquiry that they understand the duty to tell the truth
Any witness of fact	Hearsay rule not applicable in family proceedings. Witness may not give opinions.
An expert witness	May give fact and opinion, can refer to charts, notes, tables and reference works

ANY WITNESS MAY PRODUCE ALL OR ANY OF THESE:

Photographs	Provided produced by taker, who has unretouched negatives and can produce originals
Tape recordings	Provided shown to be original and not tampered with
X-rays	As photographs
Other objects	eg clothing, weapons, admissible provided relevant
Video recordings	If of an incident, admissible as photograph. Admissibility and content of interviews may be questioned

Notes may be used provided that They were made contemporaneously with events, or sufficiently soon thereafter for the memory of the person making the note to be clear

DOCUMENTARY EVIDENCE:

May be admissible provided it complies with s 1 Evidence Act 1938. Personal knowledge of facts/or statement of fact is or forms part of continuous record in which the maker recorded facts given by another who had personal knowledge of them and maker gives evidence. Medical notes come into this category. Special rules for computer records. Copies may be accepted for same reason if certified to be true copies. Documents copied by the GAL may be adduced in evidence, s 42 CA 1989

SELF-PRODUCING DOCUMENTS:

Memorandum of conviction	Admissible under s 7(2) of the Rehabilitation of Offenders Act 1974, Sched 13 of the Children Act 1989, and s 73 of the Police and Criminal Evidence Act 1984, and Home Office Circulars 88/1982; 105/1982; and 102/1988, and see Police Act 1997, Pt V.
School attendance records	Admissible under s 95 Education Act 1944
Medical certificate	Admissible under s 26 CYPA 1963.

11.6.1 Notes of evidence

There is a duty on the court to take a note of the 'substance of oral evidence given' at the proceedings, r 20 Family Proceedings (Children Act 1989) Rules 1991 and r 4.20 Family Proceedings Rules 1991.

11.6.2 Order of evidence

Rule 21(2) Family Proceedings (Children Act 1989) Rules 1991 and r 4.21(2) Family Proceedings Rules 1991 empower the court to regulate its own proceedings, for example, vary the order of speeches and evidence to suit the needs of the case and the people involved.

Unless the courts do create a variation of procedure, r 21(3) and r 4.21(3) respectively set out the order of evidence as follows:

(a) applicant;

(b) any party with parental responsibility for the child;

(c) other respondents (including a child who is separately represented);

(d) the guardian ad litem;

(e) the child, if he is not a party and there is no guardian ad litem.

(This is an unusual situation which would apply in private law cases, since in most Pt IV CA 1989 cases there is a guardian ad litem appointed and a child of sufficient age to instruct a lawyer separately will be a party.)

11.6.3 Extent of evidence

There are some limitations on the courts regulating their own proceedings. They must hear some evidence, even if the matter is agreed. It is not normally sufficient to file statements and to rely on these to support a case, calling no oral evidence at all, although this may occur in exceptional circumstances. In *Re B (Minors) (Contact)* [1994] 2 FLR 1, Butler-Sloss LJ in the Court of Appeal, hearing an issue of defined contact, gave guidance to the courts on approaching the matter of how much evidence is appropriate, p 6A(1)–(6).

In *Re F (Minor) (Care Order: Procedure)* [1994] 1 FLR 240 a magistrates' court which had heard evidence from the local authority but refused to hear the evidence of the father was held to be quite wrong. The justices should have heard the evidence from both sides. In *S v Merton LBC* [1994] 1 FCR 186, a family proceedings court was criticised for making its decision on submissions only and it was held that some evidence at least is required!

Directions hearing checklist

- **List of witnesses**
- **Dates to avoid**
  - parties
  - witnesses of fact
  - expert witnesses
  - advocate's engagements
- **Information and assistance for court proceedings**
  - reference material
  - exhibits
  - interpreter
  - visual aids in court
  - TV links; tape recorder/player
  - security
  - wheelchair access
  - hearing loop, etc
- **Information for expert witnesses**
  - documents in case, and/or list
    (leave required for disclosure to expert)
  - exhibits to be sent to expert or in expert's possession
  - chronology
  - arrangements for conference of experts
- **Leave of the court or consents necessary**
  - disclosure of documents, information, exhibits
  - medical or psychiatric examinations and their venue, who will accompany child, to whom results are to be given
  - bloods or other special testing (does it need High Court consent, for example HIV?)
  - excuse party/child attendance at court
  - accommodation of child
  - withholding information from party (High Court consent)

- **Statements and reports to be filed with the court**
  - ○ parties; witnesses; experts; chronology; reports; other documents from files
- **Statements or reports late?**
  - ○ consent of the court required for late filing
- **Service**
  - ○ applicant and parties; those entitled to notice of the proceedings; those entitled to be respondents; guardian ad litem; others

11.7   Courtroom skills

11.7.1   Court manners

Proceedings are non-adversarial, and in an inevitably emotional situation, a calm advocate can assist everyone greatly in family proceedings.

Titles

Magistrates	Your Worship, Sir or Madam
Deputy/District Judge	Sir or Madam
County Court Judge	Your Honour
High Court and Court of Appeal Judges	My Lord or My Lady (usually pronounced by the Bar as M'Lord or M'Lady)
Barristers and solicitors referring to each other	My friend, Counsel for X or Mr, Mrs or Ms ...

The applicant's advocate introduces other advocates and parties to the court. Find out their names before going in. Greet other parties and advocates on arrival at court, letting the court usher know of your arrival. Ushers enter the names of everyone present on their court list. Stand while the judge or bench enters the room, and allow them to sit before sitting yourself. Figure 7, opposite, illustrates a typical family proceedings courtroom layout and seating.

Figure 7: Layout of typical family proceedings court

WITNESS BOX

THE MAGISTRATES BENCH		
MAGISTRATE	CHAIRPERSON	MAGISTRATE

MAGISTRATES' CLERK				SOLICITOR FOR THE LOCAL AUTHORITY
GUARDIAN AD LITEM				SOCIAL WORKER
SOLICITOR FOR THE CHILD				EXPERT WITNESS
CHILD, IF PRESENT AT COURT				EXPERT WITNESS
SOLICITOR FOR PARENT	PARENT	SOLICITOR FOR PARENT	PARENT	

Notes:
The seating plan is flexible. Parents may not wish to sit together if separately represented. A child, if present, may not wish to sit next to parents.
Witnesses may sit or stand to give evidence.

The family proceedings courts and county courts may conduct their proceedings seated. Check with the clerk to the court. The general rule for advocates or witnesses is to stand until invited to sit.

Don't interrupt another advocate when addressing the court. Allow them to finish, then request the court's permission to correct factual or legal errors. Making audible critical 'asides' to other advocates or clients is not acceptable, and is unprofessional.

Bring to court sufficient spare copies of documents and draft orders for all the parties who need to have one. The original goes to the judge or bench, with a copy to the clerk.

The examination of witnesses follows the order of evidence (see above). Each witness is called to the witness box by the party calling him, sworn in or requested to affirm and then examined in chief. Questions which suggest an answer are 'leading questions' and forbidden in examination in chief; one must not 'lead the witness'. For example, ask 'What time of day was it?' not 'Was it three o'clock?'

The other parties may then cross-examine the witness. Finally, the party calling the witness may re-examine to clarify points already made. The court should then be offered the opportunity to ask questions of the witness. Ask permission before the witness leaves the court, if not required further.

Traditionally, the applicant opens the case and outlines their case to the court. The other parties then have the opportunity to make a speech to the court but usually do so at the end of the case. The guardian ad litem or their advocate will be the last to speak. If there are submissions on law during the case, the order of address follows the order of evidence.

When the case is completed, stand for the magistrates or judge to leave the room before the advocates.

These notes are necessarily brief, but there are many good books and courses on advocacy, and by far the best way of learning courtroom skills is to sit in on cases with experienced Children Panel advocates – not to copy them, but to learn by observation and to develop our own individual strengths and skills as advocates.

12 Children's Rights

The law affecting the rights of children includes: the Children Act 1989 (the 'Children Act'); the UN Convention on the Rights of the Child (in force in the UK on 15 January 1992); the Human Rights Act 1998 (in force in the UK from 2 October 2000); and the European Convention for the Protection of Human Rights and Fundamental Freedoms (ECHR) and its Protocols. Other legislation affords specific rights to children and families, for example Mental Health and is cited below where relevant.

Under s 22(4) of the Human Rights Act 1998, all proceedings brought by a public authority are subject to the ECHR, even where the alleged breach of these rights occurred before the coming into force of the Human Rights Act.

It is important to make a clear distinction between two situations in which consent may be required. The first is where doctors seek to carry out diagnostic assessments which may be necessary before deciding on the best method of treatment, and/or medical, psychiatric, or psychological treatments necessary to maintain the child's health and welfare.

The second category is where medical, psychiatric or psychological assessments are sought for purely forensic purposes.

Depending on the child's age and other considerations, in special circumstances the courts may overrule a child's refusal of necessary treatment, but the courts will be far less willing to overrule a child's refusal of an assessment for forensic purposes.

12.1 To accept or refuse medical treatment

No adult or child competent to make their own medical decisions may be given medical treatment without their consent. Treatment without consent (save in emergencies) may incur liability for damages for assault, or constitute an offence in criminal law. Detention in hospital or any other place without consent could constitute false imprisonment.

The issue therefore, is at what age can a child give valid consent?

12.1.1   Children over the age of 16 (but under 18)

Under s 8 of the Family Law Reform Act 1969, at the age of 16, a young person gains the right to give informed consent to surgical, medical or dental treatment. Examinations or assessments must impliedly be included. The consent of the young person is as valid as that of an adult. A young person with mental illness, disability, or psychiatric disturbance is subject to the Mental Health Acts.

If a young person consents to recommended medical or dental treatment, therefore, (even if their parents disagreed for some reason) the medical or dental practitioner would be protected from a claim for damages for trespass to the person.

However, if the young person refuses recommended treatment, although those with parental responsibility for the young person may give a valid consent which will have the effect of protecting the medical or dental practitioner from claims for damages for trespass to the person; it should be noted that as the age of the young person increases towards 18, their refusal and the reasons for it are important considerations for parents and the court.

In the event of a dispute about consent for medical treatment, the issue should be taken before the High Court, either under its inherent jurisdiction or under s 8 of the Children Act for a specific issue order. In the case of *Re W (A Minor) (Consent to Medical Treatment)* [1993] 1 FLR 1 the Court of Appeal gave consent for the treatment of a girl of 16 with anorexia nervosa, despite her refusal.

In circumstances requiring sterilisation; termination of a pregnancy; or surgical interventions to save or prolong the child's life, if the child is a ward of court, the High Court's consent is required.

If parents refuse to allow medical treatment and a child needs it, the High Court can provide the requisite authority under its inherent jurisdiction.

12.1.2   Children under 16

The legal situation for consent by children under 16 but who are judged to be 'Gillick competent' is similar to that of young people over 16, described in 12.1.1 above. For those who are not considered to be Gillick competent, decisions concerning medical treatment are made for them by those with parental responsibility and, where necessary, the courts will intervene or assist in the ways described above.

In Gillick v West Norfolk and Wisbech AHA [1986] AC 112 the House of Lords formulated the concept now known colloquially as 'Gillick competence' in which the ability of a child under 16 to make her own medical decisions is evaluated according to chronological age considered in conjunction with the child's mental and emotional maturity, intelligence and comprehension.

Lord Scarman said:

> It will be a question of fact whether a child seeking advice has sufficient understanding of what is involved to give a consent valid in law. Until the child achieves the capacity to consent, the parental right to make the decision continues save only in exceptional circumstances. Emergency, parental neglect, abandonment of the child, or inability to find the parent are examples of exceptional situations ...

Gillick competence has been reviewed in a number of subsequent cases. In Re S (Minor) (Refusal of Treatment) [1995] 1 FCR 604 it was held that a girl of almost 16 suffering from thalassaemia major should continue with her treatment, despite her refusal to do so on religious grounds. The discontinuance of treatment would have resulted in her death within a few weeks. The court acknowledged that at 18 she could refuse and effectively end her life, but expressed the hope that in the intervening period she might change her mind, or that gene therapy would relieve her condition.

See also Re L (Medical Treatment: Gillick Competency) [1998] 2 FLR 810, and Re M (Child:Refusal of Medical Treatment) [1999] 2 FCR 577, where a heart transplant was authorised for a 15 year old girl.

Understanding the potential consequences of refusing treatment or assessment increases with age and maturity, and the child's intelligence and level of understanding, influenced by the detail of the information provided. The National Health Service Guide to Consent for Examination or Treatment (1990) HC (90) 22 recommends that doctors should record factual information given to the child, including questions asked and the child's responses, for possible reference later if the child's ability to make the decision were to be questioned. Where a child is seen alone, efforts should be made to obtain the child's agreement to inform their parents, save where this is clearly not in the child's best interests.

For medical and psychiatric treatment in the context of supervision orders, see below, 12.2.1.

12.1.3   Mentally disordered children

Where a child is mentally ill or mentally disordered and unable to make a legally valid decision for himself, the High Court in its wardship jurisdiction may consent on behalf of a person under 18. The High Court may order reasonable force to be used to ensure compliance, see *A Metropolitan Borough Council v DB* [1997] 1 FLR 767 .

The safeguards in the Mental Health Act 1983 apply. Section 131(2) allows parents to arrange for the informal admission of children under 16 to hospital for treatment for mental disorder, the admission of those over 16 if they are incapable of making their own decisions or expressing their own wishes. The definition of 'nearest relative' in s 27(2) of the Mental Health Act 1983 is now amended to substitute for the word 'mother', mother and father with parental responsibility.

12.1.4   Where nobody has parental responsibility

In situations where an immediate decision or action is needed and no one with parental responsibility is available, s 3(5) of the Children Act provides:

> a person who:
>
> (a)   does not have parental responsibility for a particular child; but
>
> (b)   has care of the child,
>
> may ... do what is reasonable in all the circumstances of the case for the purpose of safeguarding or promoting the child's welfare.

This section was intended for use by neighbours, relatives, or others looking after children who may need to take the child urgently to the GP or dentist, but should not be used to give consent for major medical decisions.

12.2 To accept or refuse medical or psychiatric assessment

Child protection often necessitates medical or psychiatric examination or assessment. The *Report of the Inquiry into Child Abuse in Cleveland,*

1987, London: HMSO, demonstrated that repeated medical examinations can themselves be abusive. The court has wide power to set limits by directions, for example, the place and time of an examination; person(s) to be present; person(s) to conduct the examination; and person(s) or authorities to whom the results shall be given.

12.2.1 Circumstances in which the court may direct medical or psychiatric examination or assessment which the child has a right to refuse

In the following circumstances, a child of sufficient understanding has the right to refuse consent to medical or psychiatric examination:

(a) interim care order, s 38(6) of the Children Act;

(b) interim supervision order, s 38(6) of the Children Act;

(c) emergency protection order, s 44(6)(b) and (7) of the Children Act;

(d) child assessment order, s 43(8) of the Children Act.

In supervision orders, the child may be directed to undergo a medical, but not a psychiatric examination, but (where the child has sufficient understanding to exercise their right of consent) the court may only make this direction if the child consents, see para 4, Sched 3 to the Children Act. The court may order psychiatric treatment of a child under a supervision order in specified circumstances, or medical treatment, and, again, consent is required of a child who has sufficient understanding to exercise their right of consent, see para 5, Sched 3 to the Children Act.

Where the child has the right to refuse medical or psychiatric examinations, his wishes and feelings must be ascertained by the guardian ad litem, or doctor, see paras 3.50–3.51 *The Children Act 1989 Guidance and Regulations,* Vol 1, *Court Orders.*

Doctors must check whether the child is capable of giving an informed decision, and that he consents, before proceeding with an examination. Even if the court has directed an examination with the child's consent, if, when the child is with the doctor he then refuses, the doctor should not proceed, but should refer the matter back to the court. If the court agrees that this is an informed decision, then usually the court will respect the refusal, but if the refusal may place the child in serious danger, then it is possible that the High Court may overrule the refusal in the child's best interests. Such an event would be very rare.

12.3 To make his or her own application to the court

Under s 10(8) of the Children Act, children of sufficient age and understanding may make their own applications for s 8 orders, with leave of the court. Note that all applications by a child for leave to seek a s 8 order should be heard in the High Court – *Practice Direction* [1993] 1 All ER 820; [1993] 1 FLR 668.

Following *Re SC (Minor) (Leave to Seek Residence Order)* [1994] 1 FLR 96, where the child is the applicant, then his welfare is paramount, because the provisions of s 10(9) Children Act 1989 do not apply. (Section 10(9) of the Children Act sets out the criteria for the court's consideration in granting leave for all other applicants, and it has been held that the child's welfare is not paramount in those applications.) Also, everyone with parental responsibility for the child should have notice of the application (see 13.2.2 below).

Children may seek other orders under the Children Act, with leave, including discharge of:

(a) care;

(b) supervision;

(c) emergency protection;

(d) s 8 orders;

(e) parental responsibility orders;

(f) parental responsibility agreements.

The decision as to whether a child is of sufficient age and understanding to apply is a matter initially for the solicitor instructed by the child, but ultimately for the court to decide *Re CT (Minor) (Wardship: Representation)* [1993] 3 WLR 602; [1993] 2 FLR 278. The court could appoint a next friend for the child, usually the Official Solicitor, under rr 9.2A(10)(b) and 9(5) Family Proceedings Rules 1991.

12.4 To request confidentiality and, in the event of disagreement with the guardian ad litem, to instruct a solicitor separately

Where children are subject to care or supervision applications, the child has a solicitor appointed for them by the guardian ad litem or the court. The child's solicitor takes instructions from the guardian ad litem and from the child. A child of sufficient age and understanding may request client confidentiality with their solicitor on specific issues, or generally.

A child of sufficient age and understanding may disagree with the recommendations of the guardian ad litem, remaining a party with his own solicitor. The guardian will notify the court and continue unrepresented, or appoint another solicitor. Procedure is governed by rr 11(3), 12(1)(a), and 12(3)–(5) Family Proceedings (Children Act 1989) Rules; and rr 4.11(3), 4.12(1)(a), and 4.12(3)-(5) Family Proceedings Rules 1991. The ethics, duties and responsibilities of the solicitor for the child are discussed in Chapter 16 below.

12.5 Rights of a child in care

A child in care has rights protected by the Children Act and also by the Guidance issued under it. The child has a right to:

(a) refuse medical or psychiatric assessment ordered within an interim care order under s 38(6) of the Children Act;

(b) refuse medical or psychiatric assessment in specified circumstances, see above, 12.2;

(c) reasonable contact with his family, see above, 7.6.4. and paras 9 and 13–16 of *The Care of Children, Principles and Practice in Regulations and Guidance* (1991, London: HMSO) ('*Principles and Practice*');

(d) be consulted on issues involving her care, see paras 2.21 and 6.4, *Guidance and Regulations* Vol 3; also paras 2.21, 2.45, *Guidance and Regulations* Vol 4, ss 22(4), 61 and 64 of the Children Act and para 25, *Principles and Practice;*

(e) have his race, culture, religion and background taken into account in care proceedings, s 1 Children Act and para 4, *Principles and Practice;*

(f) consult a solicitor of her own if of sufficient age and understanding, see above, 12.4;

(g) develop a sense of identity, para 19, *Principles and Practice;*

(h) grow to independence, para 26, *Principles and Practice;*

(i) to live in peace and safety, free from abuse, para 3, *Principles and Practice* and Art 3, ECHR;

(j) regular reviews of his care plan and involvement in the planning in a way appropriate to his age and understanding, paras 3.8, 3.11(a), 3.15, *Guidance and Regulations* Vol 4;

(k) the child's wishes should also be taken into account when planning for placements and for future care, para 3.20, also ss 22(4), 61 and 64 of the Children Act and para 25, *Principles and Practice;*

(l) the right to 'family life', Art 8, ECHR, relevant to contact;

(m) the right to liberty and security, Art 5, ECHR;

(n) the right not to be treated in an inhuman and degrading way, Art 6, ECHR;

(o) the right to a 'fair trial', Art 6, ECHR – relevant to forensic evidence, conduct of hearings, admission of evidence. This right could extend to exclusion of a child from a decision making by local authorities and others;

(p) the rights conferred on children under 18 years in the UN Convention on the Rights of the Child.

13 Other Children Act Orders Available to the Court in Family Proceedings

The Children Act 1989 (the 'Children Act') empowers the court to make certain orders of its own volition in 'family proceedings', defined in s 8(3) and s 105 of the Children Act as amended by subsequent legislation. There is a 'menu' of orders available in family proceedings (see below, Figure 8) from which the court may choose, subject to the principles of s 1 of the Children Act. Note that the court should make no order unless it is necessary for the welfare of the child, see Chapter 2. The court cannot, however, intervene in family proceedings to impose orders for care, supervision, secure accommodation, emergency protection or child assessment.

13.1 Orders in family proceedings

Family proceedings, and the 'menu' of orders available, are shown in Figure 8. Family Assistance Orders require no application, but the parties must agree to their making. Note also that in the magistrates court, unlike the other courts, all proceedings under the Children Act are classed as family proceedings under s 92(2) of the Children Act. Save in the magistrates court, the following orders under the Children Act are not classed as family proceedings: emergency protection order, child assessment order and recovery orders.

Figure 8: Menu of orders available in family proceedings

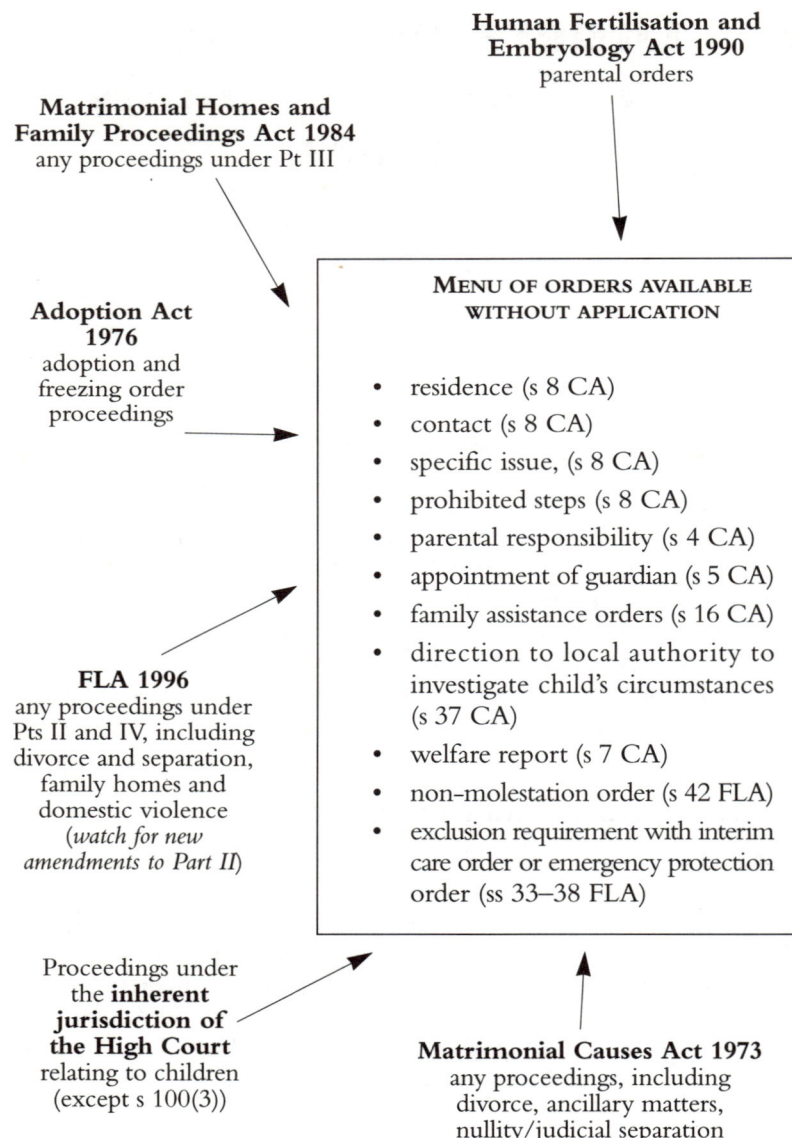

Human Fertilisation and Embryology Act 1990
parental orders

Matrimonial Homes and Family Proceedings Act 1984
any proceedings under Pt III

Adoption Act 1976
adoption and freezing order proceedings

FLA 1996
any proceedings under Pts II and IV, including divorce and separation, family homes and domestic violence
(*watch for new amendments to Part II*)

Proceedings under the **inherent jurisdiction of the High Court**
relating to children (except s 100(3))

Matrimonial Causes Act 1973
any proceedings, including divorce, ancillary matters, nullity/judicial separation

MENU OF ORDERS AVAILABLE WITHOUT APPLICATION

- residence (s 8 CA)
- contact (s 8 CA)
- specific issue, (s 8 CA)
- prohibited steps (s 8 CA)
- parental responsibility (s 4 CA)
- appointment of guardian (s 5 CA)
- family assistance orders (s 16 CA)
- direction to local authority to investigate child's circumstances (s 37 CA)
- welfare report (s 7 CA)
- non-molestation order (s 42 FLA)
- exclusion requirement with interim care order or emergency protection order (ss 33–38 FLA)

Note: 'Family proceedings' are defined in ss 8(3) and 105 Children Act 1989, are 'family proceedings' but, in other courts. emergency protection proceedings'.

Part II Children Act 1989
s 8 orders:
contact
prohibited steps
residence
specific issue
change of surname (s 13)
removal from jurisdiction (s 13)
family assistance orders (s 16)

Crime and Disorder Act 1998
Proceedings under ss 11 and 12 for safety orders

MENU OF ORDERS AVAILABLE ONLY ON APPLICATION

Children Act 1989
all cases in the magistrates' courts (s 92(2))

- termination of parental responsibility (s 4 CA)
- financial provision (s 15 CA)
- care or supervision order (s 31 CA)
- education supervision order (s 36 CA)
- child assessment order (s 43 CA)
- emergency protection order (s 44 CA)
- recovery order (s 50 CA)
- child safety order (ss 11–12 CDA)
- occupation order (ss 33–38 FLA)

Part I Children Act 1989
parental responsibility (ss 2–4)
guardianship (ss 5 and 6)

Part IV Children Act 1989
care (s 31)
supervision (s 35)
care contact orders (s 34)
education supervision order (s 36)

Domestic Proceedings, Magistrates' Courts Act 1978
maintenance of partners and children

as amended. All cases in the magistrates' court, under the Children Act 1989 orders, child assessment orders and recovery orders are not classed as 'family

13.2 Section 8 orders

Section 8(1)of the Children Act creates the s 8 orders: contact, prohibited steps, residence and specific issue, all available in all family proceedings. The court may regulate, on an application or of its own volition, the child's residence and contact with others; prohibit specified steps without leave of the court; and deal with any specific issues arising in the child's upbringing.

Some applicants are entitled to apply, and others must first seek the leave of the court. The following are entitled under s 10 of the Children Act to apply for any s 8 order:

(a) any parent or guardian of a child, s 10(4)(a) (this will include the unmarried father of a child whether or not he has parental responsibility);

(b) any person in whose favour a residence order is in force with respect to the child, s 10(4)(b).

The following are entitled to apply for a residence or contact order (but not a prohibited steps order or a specific issue order):

(a) any party to a marriage (whether or not subsisting) in relation to whom the child is a child of the family, s 10(5)(a) (this provision enables a stepparent to seek a residence or contact order);

(b) any person with whom the child has lived for a period of at least three years, s 10(5)(b) (s 10(10) provides that the three year period need not be continuous but must have begun not more than five years before, or ended more than three months before, the making of the application);

(c) • any person who, where there is a residence order in force with respect to the child, has the consent of each of the persons in whose favour the order is made, s 10(5)(c)(i);

• any person who, where there is a care order in force, has the consent of the local authority, s 10(5)(c)(ii) (but note, the court can only make a residence order in such circumstances);

• any person who, in any other case, has the consent of each of those (if any) with parental responsibility for the child, s 10(5)(c)(iii).

13.2.1 Leave to apply

Any other person needs leave to apply for a s 8 order, including the child. The court must be satisfied that a child applicant has sufficient understanding to make the proposed application, and the application must be made to the High Court, see *Practice Direction* [1993] 1 All ER 820. The Court of Appeal has said that this is a 'serious step' which should not be taken lightly. An application by a child in statutory care for a residence order, if successful, would have the effect of discharging the care order.

Note that in *Re A (Care: Discharge Application by a Child)* [1995] 1 FLR 599 Thorpe J held that a child's application to discharge care was not one which required leave of the court.

13.2.2 Considerations on application for leave

Section 10(9) requires that on applications for leave the court should have regard to various considerations which do not include the paramountcy principle. On the issue of leave, the welfare of the child is not of paramount importance because an application for leave is not a trial of the substantive issue, see *North Yorkshire CC v G* [1993] 2 FLR 732. If, however, the child is the applicant, then s 10(9) does not apply, see *Re C (Minor) (Leave to Seek s 8 Order)* [1994] 1 FLR 96.

Section 10(9) sets out the matters to be taken into account:

(a) the nature of the proposed application;

(b) the applicant's connection with the child;

(c) any risk that there might be of that proposed application disrupting the child's life to such an extent that he would be harmed by it; and

(d) where the child is being looked after by a local authority:

- the authority's plans for the child's future; and
- the wishes and feelings of the child's parents.

13.2.3 Duration

Section 8 orders subsist until the child reaches 16, unless they are brought to an end earlier by the court, or made of limited duration, s 91(11) of the Children Act. They may in exceptional circumstances be extended until the child reaches 18 years of age, s 9(6) of the Children Act.

There is no such animal under the Children Act as an 'interim s 8 order' but instead, only a full order of limited duration, see *S v S (Custody:Jurisdiction)* [1995] 1 FLR 155 and also *Re M (Official Solicitor's Role)* [1998] 2 FLR 815.

13.2.4 When the court may not make a s 8 order

(a) Section 9(1) Children Act establishes restrictions on making s 8 orders:

No court shall make any s 8 order, other than a residence order, with respect to a child who is in the care of a local authority.

A residence order will result in the automatic discharge of the care order, s 91(1) of the Children Act. A care order automatically discharges a s 8 order, s 91(2) of the Children Act.

(b) Section 9(2) states:

No application may be made by a local authority for a residence order or contact order and no court shall make such an order in favour of a local authority.

(c) Section 9(3) imposes restrictions on the application to the court for leave to apply for s 8 orders by some foster parents.

All foster parents need leave of the court to apply for a s 8 order unless they are entitled to apply. If they have fostered the child within the preceding six months they will need the consent of the local authority before seeking leave to apply unless they are related to the child, or the child has lived with them for a period exceeding three years.

(d) Section 9(4) goes on to provide that 'the period of three years ... need not be continuous, but must have begun not more than five years before the making of the application'.

(e) Section 9(5)(a) forbids a court to make a specific issue or prohibited steps order 'with a view to achieving a result which could be achieved by making a residence or contact order'.

Specific issue and prohibited steps orders are regarded as quite formidable powers, to be used sparingly and only where appropriate:

(a) Section 9(5)(b) forbids a court to exercise its power to make a specific issue or prohibited steps order *'in any way which is denied to the High Court (by s 100(2)) in the exercise of its inherent jurisdiction with respect to children'*.

(b) The essential purpose of s 100(2) of the Children Act is to ensure that local authorities seeking some measure of control over a child do so by way of proceedings under Pts IV or V of the Act and not by invoking wardship. Section 9(5)(b) of the Children Act applies the same principle to s 8 proceedings.

(c) Section 9(6) prohibits the making of any s 8 order which is to have effect for a period which will end after the child has reached the age of 16, unless the circumstances are exceptional. An application in respect of a child with severe learning difficulties or physical mobility problems may well constitute an exception.

13.3   Contact

A contact order means an order requiring the person with whom a child lives, or is to live, to allow the child to visit the person named in the order, or for that person and the child otherwise to have contact with each other.

This order governs contact by direct and indirect means, including visits, staying over, telephone calls, tapes, videos, letters, cards and presents.

Contact orders generally will expire when the child reaches 16, unless there are exceptional circumstances. Contact orders lapse if the parents live continuously together for more than six months, s 11(6) of the Children Act.

13.4   Prohibited steps

A prohibited steps order means an order that no step which could be taken by a parent in meeting his parental responsibility for a child, and which is of a kind specified in the order, shall be taken by any person without the consent of the court. This order enables the court to spell out those matters which are to be referred back to it for a decision.

13.5   Residence

A residence order means an order settling the arrangements to be made as to the person with whom the child is to live. Section 11(4) Children Act empowers the court to specify periods of residence in each household involved and for all s 8 orders, under s 11(7), the court may make conditions and directions if necessary to facilitate the implementation of the order.

13.5.1   Residence orders and parental responsibility

Residence orders do not remove parental responsibility from anyone else who has it. Parental responsibility can be given to the person in whose favour a residence order is made, remaining while the order is in force, s 12(2) of the Children Act, and see above, Chapter 4. Residence orders generally expire when the child reaches 16, unless there are exceptional circumstances, see 13.2.3 above.

Section 12(1) specifically requires the court to make an order under s 4 giving parental responsibility to a father in favour of whom it makes a residence order if he would not otherwise have it. The court may not bring that parental responsibility order to an end while the residence order remains in force, s 12(4). There is an additional effect of the combined operation of s 12(2) and (4) for an unmarried father, which is that discharge of the residence order, or its expiry by effluxion of time will not automatically result in the discharge of his parental responsibility for his child. He continues by implication to have parental responsibility for his child until the child reaches 18, unless it is specifically discharged by court order under s 4(4).

The Act does not allow parental responsibility given under this section to cover agreement to adoption, or a s 18 Adoption Act 1976 application, nor does it permit the appointment of a guardian for the child, s 12(3) of the Children Act.

Section 13(1)(b) of the Children Act generally prohibits the removal of a child from the United Kingdom without the written consent of every person who has parental responsibility for the child, or the leave of the court; whilst s 13(2) makes an exception permitting a person in whose favour a residence order is made to take the child abroad for a period of less than one month.

A parent who fears that a child may be removed abroad permanently on the pretext of a short holiday may apply for a prohibited steps order excluding the effect of s 13(2). Where the question of the removal of the child from the jurisdiction is anticipated the court may on the making of a residence order give leave either generally, or for specified purposes, s 13(3).

Where a child is subject to a residence order or to a care order, no person may change that child's surname without the written consent of every person with parental responsibility for that child, or leave of the court, s 13(1)(a) of the Children Act.

13.6 Specific issue

A specific issue order means an order giving directions for the purpose of determining a specific issue which has arisen, or which may arise, in connection with any aspect of parental responsibility for a child.

This order enables either parent to submit a particular dispute to the court for resolution in accordance with the child's best interests. The order was not envisaged as a way of giving one parent the right to determine issues in advance, nor was it intended to be a substitute for a residence or contact order.

13.7 Supplementary provisions

Section 11(1) instructs the court to 'draw up a timetable with a view to determining the question without delay' and 'to give such directions as it considers appropriate for the purpose of ensuring, so far as is reasonably practicable, that the timetable is adhered to'.

Section 11(2) permits rules of court to 'specify periods within which specified steps must be taken in relation to proceedings in which such questions arise' and 'to make other provision ... for the purpose of ensuring, so far as is reasonably practicable, that such questions are determined without delay', see the Family Proceedings Courts (Children Act 1989) Rules 1991 and the Family Court Rules 1991.

Section 11(4) and (5) state:

Where a court has power to make a s 8 order, it may do so at any time in the course of the proceedings in question, even though it is not in a position to dispose finally of those proceedings.

Where a residence order is made in favour of two or more persons who do not themselves live together, the order may specify the periods during which the child is to live in the different households concerned [s 11(4)].

Where there is a residence order in force, as a result of which the child lives, or is to live, with one of two parents who each have parental responsibility for him, the residence order shall cease to have effect if the parents live together for a continuous period of more than six months [s 11(5)].

Section 11(6) states:

A contact order which requires the parent with whom a child lives to allow the child to visit, or otherwise have contact with, his other parent shall cease to have effect if the parents live together for a continuous period of more than six months.

Section 8 orders may contain directions, impose conditions, be made for a specified period, or contain provisions for a specified period; and make such incidental, supplemental or consequential provisions as the court thinks fit, s 11(7).

13.8 Practice and procedure in s 8 applications

Procedure is governed in the magistrates' court by the Family Proceedings (Children Act 1989) Rules 1991 SI 1991/1395 (FP(CA)R 1991) and in the county court and High Court by the Family Proceedings Rules 1991 SI 1991/1247 (FPR 1991).

13.8.1 Applications

Freestanding applications should be on form C1, or on form C2 if the application is made in existing 'family proceedings', Sched 1 FP(CA)R 1991 and App 1 FPR 1991.

If the application is for leave only, then, unless it is *ex parte* (see below, 18.6), the applicant for leave needs to complete form C2 giving reasons for the application and requesting leave in writing; and to file and serve the request together with the draft of the application on form C1 to each respondent, see r 3(1) FP(CA)R 1991 and r 4.3(1) FPR 1991.

13.8.2 Venue

Applications may be made at any level. Venue of hearings is governed by the Children (Allocation of Proceedings) Order 1991 SI 1991/1677; and in adoption cases, currently by the Adoption Act 1976.

If children seek leave to apply for a s 8 order, the case should be heard in the High Court, under *Practice Direction (Children Act 1989 – Applications by Children)* [1993] 1 WLR 313; [1993] 1 All ER 820; [1993] 1 FLR 1008.

The Legal Services Commission (formerly the Legal Aid Board) will expect that, wherever possible, the case is commenced in the lowest tier, the Family Proceedings Court, and will seek justification of commencement elsewhere, if there are factors which justify transfer up.

13.8.3 Notice of application for s 8 orders

Under r 4(3) and Sched 2 col (iv) FP(CA)R 1991 and r 4.4(3) App 3 col (iv) FPR 1991, notice shall be served on:

(a) any local authority providing accommodation for the child;

(b) anyone with whom the child is living when proceedings commence;

(c) any person providing refuge in which child is staying;

(d) any person named in court order, still in effect, relating to child;

(e) any party to pending proceedings relating to the child;

(f) every person with whom applicant believes child has lived for three years prior to the application.

Notice of the proceedings is on form C6A, giving the date, time and venue of the hearing. It should be served at least 14 days before the hearing, r 4(3) FP(CA)R 1991 and r 4.4(3) FPR 1991.

13.8.4 Respondents

Under r 7(1) and Sched 2 col (iii) FP(CA)R 1991 and r 4.7(1) and App 3 col (iii) FPR 1991, the following are automatically respondents to a s 8 application:

(a) everyone with parental responsibility for the child;

(b) if a care order is in force, everyone with parental responsibility when the order was made;

(c) parties to proceedings leading to an order for which variation or discharge is now sought.

Respondents should be served with a copy of the application with the date of hearing endorsed on it, together with notice of the proceedings on form C6A. It should be served at least 14 days before the hearing, r 4(1)(b) and Sched 2 col (ii) FP(CA)R 1991 and r 4.4(1)(b), App 3 col (ii) FPR 1991, as amended.

Anyone may apply on form C2 to be joined as respondent, or may be made a respondent by court order without application, see r 7(2) and (5) and FP(CA)R 1991 and rr 4.7(2) and (5) FPR 1991. The same applies if respondents wish to be removed. If the person requesting party status has parental responsibility for the child, the court must grant their request, r 7(4) FP(CA)R 1991 and r 4.7(4) FPR 1991.

13.8.5 Service

Service can be carried out by delivery to the solicitor acting for the person to be served, personally, by document exchange, facsimile transmission, or by first class post; or by delivery to the person himself either personally or by first class post to his last known residence, r 8(1)(a) and (b) FP(CA)R 1991 and r 4.8(1)(a) and (b) FPR 1991.

The court has the power under the rules to abridge, waive or vary the manner of service, r 8(8) FP(CA)R 1991 and r 4.8(8) FPR 1991.

13.8.6 *Ex parte* procedures

These are applications made without requiring the other party/parties to attend on notice. Applications for s 8 orders may be made *ex parte* in any court, r 4(4)(a) FP(CA)R 1991 and r 4.4(4)(a) FPR 1991 but applicants will need leave of the justices clerk in the Family Proceedings Court, r 4(4)(i) FP(CA)R 1991.

Ex parte applications must be supported by the same forms (C1 or C2) which should be brought to court or, if it is a telephone application, they should be filed within 24 hours of the application. In any event, they should be served on the respondents within 48 hours of any order being made. The court has the power under the rules to give directions as to service, see below.

Ex parte residence orders are frowned upon by the courts, and in a number of decisions this has been reiterated: *Re H (A Minor) (Interim Custody)* [1991 2 FLR 411; *Re G (Minors) (ex p Interim Residence Order)* [1993] 1 FLR 910; *Re P (A Minor) (ex p Interim Residence Order)* [1993] 1 FLR 915.

Basically, *ex parte* residence orders should be reserved for extreme urgency, such as child abduction cases. The court referral procedures for urgent applications are set out in a circular from the Lord Chancellor's Department, *Guide to Listing Officers*, September 1991.

13.8.7 Withdrawal, variation, discharge and appeals

Leave of the court is necessary for withdrawal of s 8 applications (r 5 FP(CA)R 1991 and r 4.5 FPR 1991) on oral application where the guardian ad litem and the parties are present; or by written request, setting out the reasons for withdrawal, which must then be duly served. The court may permit withdrawal without a hearing if the parties have had a chance to make representations, the views of the guardian ad litem or court welfare officer have been canvassed, and the court considers it appropriate. The court may direct that a date be set for hearing the application on seven days' notice served on the parties and the guardian ad litem or court welfare officer.

Applications to vary or discharge a s 8 order may be made by those entitled to seek the original order (see 13.1–13.2 above, and applications at 13.8). The procedure is the same as the original application. Under s 91(14) of the Children Act, the court may order that no further application be made without leave.

Section 8 orders are automatically discharged by the making of a care order, or an adoption order, see s 91(2) of the Children Act.

An appeal may be lodged with the High Court under s 94(1) Children Act against a decision of a family proceedings court concerning a s 8 order. Appeals against decisions made in the county court and High Court follow the general rules and lie to the Court of Appeal.

13.9 Family assistance order

Section 16 of the Children Act creates the family assistance order, requiring a probation or local authority officer to be made available to 'advise, assist and befriend' any person named in the order, s 16(1). But note that the court can only make this order where the circumstances are exceptional, or the court has the consent of every person named in the order save the child, s 16(3).

The person to be 'advised assisted or befriended' may be the child, or his or her parent or guardian, or any person with whom the child is living or who has a contact order in respect of the child, s 16(2). It lasts for six months, or a shorter specified period, s 16(5).

The family assistance order may direct the person(s) named in the order to take whatever steps are necessary to enable the officer to be kept informed of their address, and to be allowed to visit the named person, s 16(4).

Where there is in force a family assistance order and also a s 8 order, then the officer may refer to the court the possibility of variation or discharge of the s 8 order, s 16(6). This power should obviously be of use where a family assistance order has been made at the same time as a contact order which is clearly not working.

13.10 Order to local authority to investigate under s 37 of the Children Act

Where, in any 'family proceedings', see s 8(3) of the Children Act, in which a question arises with respect to the welfare of any child, it appears to the court that it may be appropriate for a care or supervision order to be made, the court may direct the appropriate authority to undertake an investigation of the child's circumstances, s 37(1) of the Children Act.

The local authority to whom the direction is given is then under a duty to consider whether it should:

(a) apply for a care or supervision order;

(b) provide services or assistance for the child and family;

(c) take any other action in respect of the child.

If the local authority decides not to seek a care order, it shall inform the court within eight weeks from the s 37 direction of its reasons, any services or assistance provided, and any other action taken. If the decision is made to seek care or supervision, the local authority shall also consider whether it would be appropriate to review the case at a later date, and the date of any such review shall be determined.

Note that all the actions of public authorities, and their failures to act, are subject to compliance with the Human Rights Act 1998 and the European Convention for the Protection of Human Rights and Fundamental Freedoms, even if the act or omission occurred before the implementation of the Human Rights Act in the UK on 2 October 2000, s 22(4).

The decisions of local authorities may be challenged by complaint or judicial review. A decision *not* to seek a care order may now be subject to challenge under the Human Rights Act and since the courts may not initiate care proceedings, nor make a care order without a local authority application, this may provide another route for redress in situations where it is considered that a care order should have been sought.

14 Commencement and Transfer of Proceedings

14.1 General rules

Under the Family Law Act 1986, a child in respect of whom an application is made must be either ordinarily or habitually resident in England and Wales, or physically present within the jurisdiction of the court at the time of the application. The Family Law Act applies to applications under s 8 of the Children Act 1989 (the 'Children Act') and under the inherent jurisdiction of the High Court, but has been extended to care proceedings by case law.

The general rule is that private law applications under the Children Act may be made at any level of the court, subject to the restrictions of the Legal Aid Board, which would usually prefer the lower cost option.

In public law cases, the general rule is that proceedings should be commenced in the Family Proceedings Court, with specified exceptions, see 14.2 below.

The venue of hearings under the Children Act and the Adoption Act 1976 is governed by the Children (Allocation of Proceedings) Order 1991 SI 1991/1677; the Children (Allocation of Proceedings) (Appeals) Order 1991 SI 1991/1801; the Family Proceedings (Amendment) Rules 1991 SI 1991/2113; and reference may also be made to the Home Office Circular 45/91 (in *The Children Act 1989 Guidance and Regulations*, Vol 7, p 114).

A checklist of basic commencement provisions is set out at Figure 9 below.

Figure 9: Commencement of proceedings

Children Act 1989 Section	Order	Applicant	Needs leave	Form	Court can make order of own volition	Family proceedings court	County court	High Court
4	Parental responsibility	Child's father		C1 or C2		Children (Allocation of Proceedings) Order 1991 SI 1991/1677, Home Office Circular 45/91		
4(3)	Termination of PR	Person with PR / Child	✓	C1 or C2		Applicant's choice, subject to legal aid restrictions	Applicant's choice, subject to legal aid restrictions	Applicant's choice, subject to legal aid restrictions
5	Appoint Guardian	Anyone		C1 or C2	✓		Applicant's choice, subject to legal aid restrictions	Applicant's choice, subject to legal aid restrictions
6	Terminate appt of Guardian	Anyone with PR / Child	✓	C1 or C2			Applicant's choice, subject to legal aid restrictions	Applicant's choice, subject to legal aid restrictions
8	Contact	Parent / Guardian / Person with Residence Order / Party to marriage / Person with care of child for 3 years or consent of those with PR	Anyone with leave may apply	C1 or C2	✓	Applicant's choice, subject to legal aid restrictions	Applicant's choice, subject to legal aid restrictions	Child's application for leave
8	Residence	Parent / Guardian / Person with residence order / Party to marriage / Person with care of child for 3 years or consent of those with PR	Anyone with leave may apply	C1 or C2	✓	Applicant's choice, subject to legal aid restrictions	Applicant's choice, subject to legal aid restrictions	Child's application for leave
8	Prohibited Steps	Parent / Guardian / Person with Residence Order	* Anyone with leave may apply	C1 or C2	✓	Applicant's choice, subject to legal aid restrictions	Applicant's choice, subject to legal aid restrictions	Child's application for leave / HIV tests / Restriction of publicity / International dimension

Children Act 1989 Section	Order	Applicant	Needs leave	Form	Court can make order of own volition	Family proceedings court	County court	High Court
8	Specific Issue	Parent Guardian Person with Residence Order	★ Anyone with leave may apply	C1 or C2	✓	Applicant's choice, subject to legal aid restrictions		Child seeks leave & able child disabled blood products use HIV tests Restriction of publicity International dimension
16	Family Assistance Order	Can only be made on the courts' volition with consent of the parties			✓	Any court		
25	Secure Accommodation	Local Authority Area Health Auth. NHS Trust Person caring in a residential home		C1 + Supplement C20		✓ E	E = EXCEPTIONS: ★ Court directed investigations ★ Pending proceedings		
31	Care Order or Supervision Order	Local Authority or NSPCC		C1, C2 + Suppl. C13		✓ E ★	Extension variation or discharge of existing order		
34	Care Contact Order	Local Authority Child Anyone with leave		C1 or C2	Court can make s 34 order along with Care Order	✓ E	May be commenced in the court in which direction given, proceedings are pending, or original order was made		
36	Education Supervision Order	Local Education Authority		Form C17 or C17A		✓ E			
43	Child Assessment Order	Local Authority or NSPCC		C1 + Suppl C16		✓ E			
44	Emergency Protection	Any Person		C1 with Suppl C11		✓ E			
50	Recovery Order	Person with PR by care order or Emergency Protection order Designated Officer		C1 with Suppl C18		✓ E			

The county courts are divided into categories, each having the power to hear specified types of case. These are Care Centres, Family Hearing Centres and also Divorce Centres. It is also important to ascertain that the court in which the case is to be heard is appropriate. In addition, it is vital to ensure that the judge has power to deal with the case. This is referred to colloquially as having a 'ticket' for the type of proceedings, for example, 'a care ticket'. To check whether a case is appropriate for a category of judge, refer to the *Family Proceedings (Allocation to Judiciary) Directions* 1993 [1993] 2 FLR 1008.

14.2 Specified exceptions to the general rules

Under the Children Act (Allocation of Proceedings) Order 1991 SI 1991/1677, public law proceedings may be commenced in the county court or the High Court if:

(a) there are proceedings pending in another court;

(b) there has been a court-directed investigation into the child's circumstances;

(c) the application is for extension, variation or discharge of an existing order.

In these circumstances the application may be made to the court in which the proceedings are pending, or the existing order was made.

14.2.1 Proceedings which must be commenced in the High Court

Case law and practice directions decree that certain proceedings need to be heard at High Court level.

Others cases which should be heard in the High Court include:

(a) applications for authorisation of the use of blood products (for example, where there is religious objection);

(b) issues regarding life saving or life prolonging surgical intervention;

(c) applications for post-adoption contact;

(d) leave to submit a child to HIV tests;

(e) contested issues concerning sterilisation or terminations of pregnancy of minors or mentally ill adults;

(f) cases concerning international issues; and

(g) matters concerning restriction of general publicity.

If a child seeks leave to apply for a s 8 order, the case should be heard in the High Court, under *Practice Direction (Children Act 1989 – Applications by Children)* [1993] 1 WLR 313; [1993] 1 All ER 820; [1993] 1 FLR 1008.

Leave to withhold information from parties is sufficiently serious to warrant High Court hearing, *Re M (Disclosure)* [1998] 2 FLR 1028.

The High Court has the power to refer some cases, with certain exceptions, back to a county court, with consent of the parties or after hearing parties' representations, see *Practice Direction* [1988] 2 All ER 103; [1988] 1 FLR 540.

14.3 Transfers

Transfers are governed generally by the Children (Allocation of Proceedings) Order 1991 SI 1991/1677.

When proceedings are commenced in one level of the court, they may be transferred up or down the tiers if necessary, subject to the restrictions on venue outlined above. The Children Act Advisory Committee produced a list of 'transfer triggers', see below. These are factors the presence of one or more of which in a case may be persuasive to the court to transfer the matter up. When transferring a case, the court must have regard to the principles in s 1 Children Act, and in particular the avoidance of delay.

14.3.1 The transfer 'trigger' list

The Children Act Advisory Committee has suggested that the presence of one of the factors listed below may give rise to transfer; the presence of two factors is rather more persuasive, and the presence of three or more trigger factors should lead to a transfer:

(a) Cases which cannot be heard on consecutive days.

(b) Analysis of conflicting expert evidence.

(c) Evaluation of psychiatric or medical evidence or allied professional evidence.

(d) Ritual or multiple sexual abuse.

(e) Issues affecting recently born babies.

(f) Multiplicity of children or parties.

(g) Involvement of more than one local authority.

(h) Confidential material evidence.

(i) Cases likely to last longer than two or three days.

(j) Where delay would occur unless transferred.

(k) Termination of contact.

(l) Conflict between guardian ad litem and child.

(m) Novel issues or facts.

(n) Conflict between protocols.

(o) Any other circumstance which makes case suitable for higher court.

14.4 Urgent applications

Subject to rules, guidance and case law on jurisdiction and venue (see paras 14.1–14.3 above), the referral procedures for urgent applications are set out in a circular from the Lord Chancellor's Department 'Guide to Listing Officers', September 1991.

Initially, in High Court level cases, under s 9 of the Supreme Court Act the matter can be released to a circuit judge approved to hear Children Act 1989 cases. Some s 9 judges have additional approval to hear care matters. If the matter can be handled by a nominated judge at the local court, this is the preferred route. As a general rule, circuits should deal with matters arising on Friday evenings, weekends, public and privilege holidays. The Royal Courts of Justice will take cases during weekday evenings and nights, and also may in special need, provide a circuit judge at weekends and public and privilege holidays.

The out of hours contact number of the Royal Courts of Justice is 0207 947 6000. The security officer will, on request, refer the caller to the urgent business officer for the day.

The urgent business officer needs to know:

(a) the type of application;

(b) circumstances of the case.

He will decide whether the case merits contacting one of the three members of the judiciary on duty, at the appropriate level, and he will then return the call within 10–15 minutes. The judge dealing with the matter will advise on how the application should be handled.

15 Working With Children

15.1 Appointment and role of the guardian ad litem

The guardian ad litem is a person appointed by the court to act for a child aged under 18 years, or an adult who needs such assistance. In cases under the Children Act 1989 (the 'Children Act'), a guardian ad litem should be appointed in 'specified family proceedings' (see s 41(6) of the Children Act and 15.1.1 below) unless satisfied that it is not necessary to do so; and may be appointed in certain non-specified proceedings.

The guardian ad litem should be independent and has a duty to investigate the circumstances of the case thoroughly, interviewing parties and witnesses and examining all available evidence. The guardian ad litem should interview all those who may be able to give relevant information about the child's life and circumstances and also the child and her family, and may request any necessary further information or assessments and then evaluate all the evidence. The guardian ad litem has a duty to advise the court of the child's wishes and feelings; to inform the court of the child's circumstances, bearing in mind the welfare check list; to evaluate all the options open to the court; and finally to advise the court on the best way forward in the interests of the child.

The Official Solicitor may be appointed as guardian ad litem, and the role of the Official Solicitor is set out in *Practice Note* [1999] 1 FLR 310.

The provisions governing the appointment and functioning of a guardian ad litem are in ss 41–42 of the Children Act and rr 10 and 11 Family Proceedings Court (Children Act) Rules 1991 SI 1991/1395 and rr 4.10 and 4.11 Family Proceedings Rules 1991 SI 1991/1247.

A child who is subject to 'specified proceedings' is entitled to free legal representation under the legal aid scheme. A solicitor may be appointed for the child by the guardian ad litem or by the court. A child of sufficient understanding may wish to choose their own solicitor, which is acceptable provided that the appointment complies with the Children Act and rules cited above.

The guardian ad litem has access under s 42(1) of the Children Act to all social work files and records and, if any of these documents are copied by the guardian ad litem, they are admissible in evidence before the court, s 42 (2). See the case of *Re T* [1994] 1 FLR 632 in which the local authority refused to disclose records of potential adopters to the guardian ad litem. The Court of Appeal held that the case records of adoption were within the definition of the documents to which the guardian ad litem should have access under the terms of s 42 of the Children Act.

Note the recent leading case of *Oxfordshire CC v P* [1995] 1 FLR 582 concerning the issue of how confidential information should be treated by guardians ad litem.

The guardian ad litem may ask for access to medical or psychiatric records of the child, and may wish to see the health records of others involved in the child's life.

The report of the guardian ad litem is confidential to the court and the parties and leave is required to disclose it to others, or to withhold information from parties. Leave to withhold information from parties is sufficiently serious to warrant High Court hearing, *Re M (Disclosure)* [1998] 2 FLR 1028.

The guardian ad litem in specified proceedings may bring applications on behalf of the child, or the child's solicitor if the child is of sufficient age in instruct separately (see 15.2 below).

Specified proceedings now include applications for parental orders under s 30 of the Human Fertilisation and Embryology Act 1990.

See also *The Children Act 1989 Guidance and Regulations* Vol 7 *Guardians ad Litem and Other Court-related Issues* (1989, London: HMSO); *The Children Act Advisory Committee Handbook of Best Practice in Children Act Cases* (1997, London: HMSO, DoH); the Law Society Family Law Committee's *Guidance for Solicitors Working with Guardians ad Litem* and, in a new edition, *Guide to Acting for Children* (2000), available from the Solicitors Family Law Association.

15.1.1 Specified proceedings

Specified proceedings are defined in s 41(6) of the Children Act.

15.1.2 CAFCASS proposals

Following a consultation paper in 1998, the Government are proposing radical changes to the family court advisory system by the target date of April 2001.

In cases involving divorce or separation, adoption and care proceedings, the Government is proposing to unify three advisory services: the Guardian ad Litem and Reporting Officer Service; the Family Court Welfare Service; and the Children's Branch of the Official Solicitor's Department. The new service will be the Children and Family Court Advisory and Support Service (CAFCASS), with the motto 'children first'.

Currently, the three services provide an estimated 45,000 reports each year on nearly 65,000 children. On 15 March 2000, the Criminal Justice and Court Services Bill was presented to Parliament, in which Chapter II contains the legislation for establishing CAFCASS.

The Guardian ad Litem Panels are at present independent, and the changes will require substantial alteration to the present system. At the time of writing, the necessary administrative arrangements have not been finalised, and are subject to discussion with all those involved.

One of the issues remaining to be settled is the contractual arrangements for guardians ad litem, most of whom are currently self-employed. There is concern amongst guardians that the current proposals will impede service delivery, rather than enhance it in the way CAFCASS has envisaged. We suggest that practitioners watch for information on the implementation of CAFCASS as it emerges.

Information can be obtained from the CAFCASS government website at www.open.gov.uk/lcd/cafcas.htm and at the website for NAGALRO (the organisation for guardians ad litem and reporting officers), www.nagalro.com.

15.2 Conflict between guardian ad litem and child

The child, if of sufficient age and understanding, may request client confidentiality with their solicitor, and/or disagree with the recommendations of the guardian ad litem, see below, 12.4.

In this case, the child's solicitor must decide (a) whether the child is of sufficient age and understanding to instruct separately, and (b) whether there is a conflict between the child and the guardian ad litem. If both factors are present, the solicitor should discuss the matter with the guardian ad litem. Under rr 11 and 12(1)(a) Family Proceedings Court (Children Act 1989) Rules 1991 SI 1991/1395 and rr 4.11 and 4.12(1)(a) Family Proceedings Rules 1991 SI 1991/1247, if a child radically disagrees with the guardian ad litem, and is able to instruct his or her own solicitor, then the court must be informed, and the solicitor continues to represent the child client. The guardian ad litem will then proceed unrepresented, or seek another lawyer where necessary.

The child of sufficient age may ask their solicitor to keep matters confidential, and disclosure is then an issue for the solicitor to decide . The Law Society (The Law Society's *Family Law Committee's Guidance for Solicitors Working with Guardians ad Litem*) allows a solicitor to breach the confidentiality of an immature child client where there is a risk of serious harm to the child or to others, but the guidance suggests that a mature (for example, *Gillick* competent) child may be entitled to confidentiality unless other siblings are at risk, or the child is in fear of their life or serious injury.

Another possible way to avoid ethical dilemmas for solicitors representing children (or adults in family matters) is to gain the client's agreement at the outset of taking instructions, that, if a concern arises of a risk of serious harm to the client or to others, the solicitor has permission to disclose the concerns to the guardian ad litem, or to an appropriate helping agency. This sort of agreement may be unfamiliar to lawyers, but often used by other professionals. Clients are usually willing to give their consent, and this avoids any ethical difficulty. Clients usually tell people they trust about their problems because they would like to have help. If they want to keep it secret, discuss their reasons for this. Are they afraid of reprisals, or possibly protecting someone else? Is there anyone else they feel they could trust with this information? Once we know what their fear is, we can talk over resources and referrals which are acceptable to the client. Their worry is often that the helping agencies, once told about it, might let them down by failing to provide the help needed. We can do something about that by agreeing to stay alongside the client and doing our best to ensure that they do receive effective and appropriate help, in the ways they feel are right for them.

15.3 Should I see my child client?

Lawyers representing children should, as a matter of good practice, meet with their child clients, unless, exceptionally, there is good reason not to do so. Necessary arrangements should be made in co-operation with the guardian ad litem, the child's parents and carers, and the local authority.

See *Acting for Children* by Christine Liddle, 1992, London: Law Society, pp 5–6:

> Although children vary in their ability to give instructions, it is still very beneficial to the solicitor's understanding of the case for him to meet his child client, whatever the age.

Legal aid in public law proceedings is granted to the child client, through the guardian ad litem. Initially, the solicitor is instructed through the guardian ad litem, but will need, as a vital part of the preparation of the case, to speak with child clients who appear to be of sufficient maturity to discover, firstly, whether the child is sufficiently mature to instruct separately if necessary, and, secondly, whether a conflict exists between the child and the guardian ad litem. The solicitor also needs to elicit the child's wishes and feelings in order to represent them to the court.

The lawyer and the guardian ad litem will work in conjunction with each other, and both will be meeting child clients:

> If a solicitor is to represent a child properly in court, it is necessary to understand the child's personality, behaviour, background and needs. This can be done through information gained by others, but it is best done at first hand. Even a small baby can non-verbally tell the observer a good deal about herself. Seeing a child in his environment and interacting with him gives not only greater understanding of the child but also a sense of involvement with the client which makes the task so much more personal, and gives encouragement to the solicitor act for the child as a person, rather than as an 'object of concern' or 'a case'.

In October 1994, the Solicitors Family Law Committee produced *Guidance for Solicitors Acting for Children under the Children Act 1989* . This guidance comments that a solicitor's professional training is not well designed to equip him or her to make an assessment of a child's understanding unaided, although solicitors, particularly those on the Children Panel, will have a certain amount of knowledge through experience and/or will have undergone some training in child development.

Clearly, the expectation is that solicitors will at least discuss the issue of competence with the experts in the case, and this principle should apply equally in public law cases. The guardian ad litem in a public law case is the first person to be consulted on the issue. Child psychologists, psychiatrists, counsellors and others working with the child will also have useful views.

'Gillick competence' evolved from the case of Gillick v West Norfolk and Wisbech HA and DSS [1986] AC 112 and is vitally important (see above, 12.1.2).

See also the Guide to Good Practice for Solicitors Acting for Children (2000, available from the Solicitors Family Law Association), E para 1:

> When acting for a child, the solicitor should always meet the child and due regard should be taken for the most appropriate setting and style for such a meeting. Interviews should be short and at the child's pace.

Pat Monro and Lis Forrester assume that solicitors will meet their child clients, adding practical advice:

> Where a young child is involved, the instructions will come from the guardian ad litem and it will usually be appropriate for the guardian ad litem to meet with the child in the first instance without the solicitor, who can be introduced at a later date. A young child will probably be confused by the introduction of a number of new faces, and therefore it is important for the guardian ad litem to get to know the child before the solicitor becomes involved.

See Monro, P and Forrester, L, The Guardian ad Litem, 1995, Bristol: Family Law, p 46.

There are very rare cases where it may be inappropriate for the solicitor to see the child, for example where the child is severely emotionally damaged and the introduction of a new face may adversely affect his therapeutic progress.

15.4 Taking instructions and communicating with children

Good communication with children is essential if instructions are to be effective. A basic understanding of child development, confidence in being with children (preferably accrued with practical experience) and integrity are vital. Children dislike being patronised, and they will see through prevarication. They deserve the respect of straight answers to any questions they ask, given in age appropriate language.

Older child clients may like to receive a letter to let them know that they have a solicitor and to provide a channel of communication which they can take up themselves if they are worried or curious about anything. A few stamped envelopes (addressed to the solicitor's office) sent with the introductory letter enable the child to write back if she wishes. It also empowers her – she has the telephone number from the letter, and also a means to write – so she will not be reliant on others to get in touch with her solicitor. Some solicitors will provide a phonecard for older children.

Many younger children like to send their solicitor a drawing, and to receive a reply is a great boost for their confidence. Space is needed on the office walls for the many drawings that inevitably accumulate!

Everyone has their own way of communicating with others, so there are no hard and fast rules, a few guidelines which may be of use are given below.

15.4.1 Communication with children

(a) Discuss the timing of the first meeting with the child with the guardian ad litem and whether to go with them on the first visit to the child.

(b) Find out what the guardian has already told the child about the case and about the role of guardian and solicitor and how much of the facts it is appropriate to tell the child or to discuss with her.

(c) Explain clearly and honestly issues of confidentiality to the child in age-appropriate language.

(d) Children do not like being patronised.

(e) Informal clothing is best, not formal or intimidating 'power dressing' clothes. Get on a level with young clients, maybe even sit on the floor to talk/play!

(f) Take a few props to help communication: a selection from these may be useful: paper, crayons or pencils (never felt tips or your best fountain pen), pipe cleaners, a glove puppet, a few small toys, a family of dolls, toy bus/car, toy telephone, etc.

But don't worry, if you don't feel at ease playing with toys, … it's also ok to just *talk* with children!

(g) Do not take sweets or food (this can upset carers, tummies, or tempers!).

(h) What does the child wish to be called? Names are important. Does the child have preferred names for himself or others?

(i) Try to understand the child, get them to talk about favourite/unfavourite television programmes, activities, pop stars, food, colours, clothes, football teams, toys, friends, people and pets.

(j) Usually, the guardian will have introduced the solicitor to the child, but if not, then, once the child is at ease, explain your role as their solicitor. Many older children have seen lawyers on television and have ideas about the legal system, varying from the Dickensian to *LA Law*! The explanation needs to be age appropriate. It could be something along these lines:

> I am your solicitor. Part of my job is to go along to the court and talk to the judge (or magistrates) and to tell them how you feel about what is happening now, and what you would like to happen. I would like to talk with you and listen to what you want to say ...

There will be much more to explain and discuss with a child client, but this is a start!

(k) Explain to the child what the proceedings are about, in an age appropriate way.

(l) Don't overtire a young child, or overstay: an hour or less is usually enough.

(m) Don't try to press a child for facts, especially about past traumatic events, as it may cause emotional distress, which their carers then have to deal with afterwards. Avoid questioning a child intrusively. Involve the child's carers if help is needed to engage the child; and end the visit if the child seems unwilling to continue. Never distress a child by being 'pushy' if they do not want to talk, or by overstaying. The guardian ad litem will assist with advice, help or, if the solicitor is unsure, a joint visit to the child can be made.

(n) A sense of calm, goodwill and appropriate humour helps!

15.5 Child development

There is not space in this book to discuss child development in any detail. There are a number of excellent reference books on the market, some of which are listed in Chapter 19 below.

The contribution by Mary Sheridan in Appendix 1 to *Assessing Children in Need and their Families* (2000, London: HMSO) contains concise, useful information on child development from birth to five years.

Another reference book often used by guardians ad litem is *Child Development – Diagnosis and Assessment* by Holt, KS, 1994, London: Butterworth Heinemann.

The *ABC of One to Seven* (1993) and the *ABC of Child Abuse* (1996), published by the British Medical Association, are useful, and many book shops carry a range of books on child development intended for parents which practitioners will find readable and helpful.

15.6 Understanding your child client – race, religion, culture and ethnicity

The welfare checklist pays attention to the child's 'physical educational and emotional needs', s 1(3)(b) of the Children Act; and 'age, sex, background and any characteristics of his which the court considers relevant', s 1(3)(d) of the Children Act.

Although the Children Act did not refer specifically to race, religion and culture, they are clearly included in these categories. If the child's background, and needs arising from it, is not clear to the solicitor and guardian ad litem, then expert assistance should be sought from someone who fully understands the child's cultural, religious and social needs. The child may also have physical needs which may have to be explained to a carer from a different culture, for example, food, religious taboos and customs, hair and skin care, etc. Quite often, behaviour which would not make sense within one culture in a given situation makes perfect sense when understood in the context of another. The court must take the child's needs fully into account when deciding the most appropriate way forward to promote and safeguard the child's welfare.

15.7 After the case is over

Children often develop a relationship of trust with their solicitor, and, whatever the outcome of the case, will frequently keep in touch. The guardian ad litem's role for the child ceases when the final order is made. By contrast, the solicitor is a continuing source of help and a useful contact in the outside world. Children will be pleased to have their own solicitor whom they can telephone or ask about problems as they arise, particularly as they reach their teenage years.

It is good to have a final visit to a child client and to let them have a business card to keep if they are old enough to use it. A few sheets of blank paper and a few stamped envelopes addressed to the solicitor can be left with the child, in case they want to write. If a child does write, or otherwise makes contact, make a point of responding immediately, and in a way appropriate for the child's age and understanding.

Children who are in care need to know their rights, and these should have been explained by the social services department. If a child is concerned about the standard of care, or has a need to complain, the solicitor may be the first person they think of to tell about their problem. Older children may at some time wish to instruct a solicitor on their own behalf to apply for a s 8 order, or to apply to discharge a care order, so it is essential to keep an avenue of communication open for them.

Often the child may be concerned about an aspect of their care, and the solicitor can perform a useful function in explaining and mediating between the child and parents or agencies when difficulties arise.

Older children on leaving care also have the right to additional services on leaving care under s 24 of the Children Act, and they may wish to seek advice about the ways in which their needs can be met.

Case records, statements and documents should be kept at least until the child reaches 21. In adoption cases, records may need to be kept longer. Check with the local panel of guardians ad litem on their recommendations. Guardians working from home may rely on the solicitor or their panel office to store papers. It goes without saying that cases are confidential and need to be kept securely.

16 Assessment of Children in Need and Care Planning

16.1 New developments and materials

Recently, the government has brought in the Quality Protects Programme, to 'ensure that referral and assessment processes discriminate effectively between different types and level of need, and produce a timely response' (John Hutton, Minister of State for Social Services, March 2000).

To facilitate the implementation of the Quality Protects Programme, the Department of Health has set up steering and advisory groups and the Departments of Health, Education, Employment and the Home Office have issued new materials to provide guidance, practice material, and training resources.

The emphasis will for the future be on evidence-based practice, and careful consideration of the needs of the individual child, with an expectation that inter-agency child protection and social work practice is based on analysis, reflection, and sound judgment in decision making.

Two major contributions to the Quality Protects Programme materials are companion volumes, *Framework for the Assessment of Children in Need and their Families* (2000, London: HMSO/DoH) and *Assessing Children in Need and Their Families – Practice Guidance* (2000, London: HMSO/DoH). Both of these are essential reference material for child protection practice.

Additional resources are the range of *Initial and Core Assessment Records* for children of different age groups and the *Family Assessment Pack of Questionnaires and Scales* (both 2000, London: HMSO/DoH).

Note that the new *Working Together to Safeguard Children* (1999, London: HMSO) replaces the old *Working Together Under the Children*

Act (1991, London: HMSO) and that the old '*Orange Book*', *Protecting Children A Guide to Social Workers Undertaking a Comprehensive Assessment* (1988), has been replaced by the new assessment guidance above, which, incidentally, still contains Mary Sheridan's useful child development charts for children from birth to five years, at Appendix 1.

The *Family Assessment Pack of Questionnaires and Scales* is a contribution to the assessment process by Cox and Bentovim, providing a set of measurement scales for different family situations including questionnaires on:

(a) strengths and difficulties (screening for emotional and behavioural problems);

(b) parenting daily hassles (screening for parenting stressors);

(c) adult well being (screening for irritability, depression and anxiety);

(d) home conditions (family cleanliness, etc);

(e) adolescent well-being (for self rating for depression);

(f) family activity (in different age bands, 2–6 and 7–12 years) (child-centredness);

(g) recent life events (life events as potential stressors);

(h) alcohol scale (screening for alcohol overuse);

(i) two more measuring instruments will be available later, the *Home Inventory* and the *Assessment of Family Competence, Strengths and Difficulties*. These will be available for practitioners and in training programmes.

Training materials

(a) *The Child's World, Assessing Children in Need, Training and Development Pack* (2000), put together by the NSPCC and the University of Sheffield, is also available from the DoH. It contains a video, training guide, and a reader.

(b) *Crossing Bridges – Training Resources for Working with Mentally Ill Parents and their Children.*

(c) *Making an Impact – Children and Domestic Violence.*

(d) *Turning Points – Resource Pack for Communicating with Children.*

(e) *In on the Act – Training Programme for Relevant Professionals.*

(f) Family Group Conferences.

(g) *Unaccompanied Asylum-Seeking Children: A Training Pack.*

(h) *Looking After Children – Training Resource Pack.*

(i) *Management and Implementation Guide.*

(j) Training Guide.

(k) Training Video.

(l) Video Notes.

(m)Reader.

(n) Demonstration Documents.

16.2 The assessment framework

A child who is at risk of harm is by definition deemed to be 'a child in need'. Therefore all the guidance materials listed above apply to children who are subject to care proceedings, and also apply to many other children who may be assessed for the provision of resources by a local authority under s 17 and Sched 2 to the Children Act 1989.

In *Assessing Children in Need and Their Families,* the assessment framework is depicted for clarity in the form of a triangle. The child and the safeguarding and promoting of his welfare is central to the assessment process. Each limb of the triangle thus represents a particular area or domain of the child's world, which is further broken down into that domain's component parts, all of which inter- relate, and all of which need careful consideration both at an individual level and then as the whole picture.

Figure 9: the child assessment framework

The key areas are:

(a) the child's developmental needs, which broadly looks at his emotional, social and behavioural development and function including a consideration of his identity. This area also considers the child's physical health, his self care skills and his educational development;

(b) the second limb considers the parenting capacity of the child's carers and as might be expected includes an appraisal of the provision of basic care, nurture, stimulation, guidance and boundaries, stability and emotional warmth;

(c) the third domain considers family and environmental factors, including the family history and functioning, the wider family, housing, employment, income, the family's social integration and the availability of community resources.

The structure of this assessment framework has been specifically designed to provide a systematic method for the gathering and analysing of information about children, in order that different types and levels of need can be more effectively identified.

Assessing Children in Need and Their Families looks also at the needs of children from other cultural and ethnic groups. The Practice Guidance points out that this assessment model is equally applicable to disabled children and their families, however the needs of the carers should be a particular factor to be taken into account.

The chapters each contain a significant body of reference material for further reading and research. The final chapter looks at resources to assist effective assessment, introducing the *Family Assessment Pack of Questionnaires and Scales,* and setting out the principles for use of the materials. The age-related set of *Assessment Records* produced by the DoH are an additional assessment tool.

See also *The Children Act Now: Messages from Research* (1999, London: HMSO/DoH), which summarises the major Department of Health commissioned studies on the Children Act.

16.3 Care planning

Practitioners should note that case law precedent has already established the requirement for a care plan in s 31 applications. The emphasis now is on the nature, format and content of the care plan.

More time is spent in the consideration of the care plan than almost any other aspect of care proceedings. It is far less likely that there will be a contest over the threshold criteria, than a dispute over the proposed plan for the child.

Practitioners need to have a copy of Local Authority Circular LAC (99) 29, entitled *Care Plans and Care Proceedings under the Children Act 1989.* Issued on the 12 August 1999, it sets out the format and content of the care plans upon which the courts expect to base their consideration of the appropriate order to make in care proceedings. The circular is issued under s 7 of the Local Authority Social Services Act 1970, which requires local authorities to act under the guidance of the Secretary of State, and it supplements Vol 3 *Residential Care*, and Vol 4 *Family Placements* of *The Children Act 1989 Guidance and Regulations.*

The circular sets out the contents of the care plan, in five sections:

(a) overall aim;

(b) child's needs including contact;

(c) views of others;

(d) placement details and timetable;

(e) management and support by local authority.

Each child must have their own individual care plan, this also applies to sibling groups. The plan must be separate document, and in the case of a final care plan should not only be signed by the social worker responsible for compiling the plan, but should also be endorsed by one or more 'relevant senior officers' from within the local authority.

The local authority should provide interim care plans in order that the court has the necessary information available before making interim orders. The circular indicates that during proceedings the numbering of care plans is desirable to reduce confusion, and to ensure that parties know which care plan is in operation.

The format of the care plan is set out in detail at paras 15–18. There is comment about care plans and assessment which relates to the new framework for the assessment of children in need (para 23), comment about the needs of disabled children (para 26), race, culture, religion and language (para 27) and care planning prior to adoption (paras 28–33).

Copies of LAC (99)29 can be obtained from the DoH, PO Box 777, London SE1 6XH, or from the website at www.open.gov.uk/ doh/dhome.htm. Other recent circulars can also be obtained from this website.

16.4 Adoption issues

Attention is drawn to Local Authority Circular LAC (98) 20 *Adoption, Achieving the Right Balance* issued in August 1998. It sets out the current thinking on avoidance of delay and, in the interests of the child, finding alternative families, and decision making in potential adoption cases.

See also *Adoption Now: Messages from Research* (1999, London: HMSO/DoH) which summarises the major Department of Health commissioned studies on adoption.

There have long been proposals for change in the field of adoption, and now the government has commissioned a review of adoption law and practice, which may bring about change in the near future. Attitudes are changing. Long term fostering as an alternative to adoption; the role of freeing orders; and post adoption contact will no doubt both be carefully considered in the review.

17 Legal Aid, Appeals and Enforcement

17.1 Legal aid

The Legal Services Commission replaced the the Legal Aid Board in April 2000, setting up a Community Legal Service under the Access to Justice Act 1999. Financial matters are governed by new sets of regulations:

- Community Legal Service (Financial) Regulations 2000 SI 2000/516;
- Community Legal Service (Cost Protection) Regulations 2000 SI 2000/824;
- Community Legal Service (Costs) Regulations 2000 SI 2000/441.

There is insufficient space here to discuss the changes in the provision of 'legal services' in detail, but basically, although the terminology has changed, the former criteria remain, in that the provision of legal services will be based on 'the prospects of success' (formerly merits of the case); the means of the client, and the type of proceedings. Decisions are made according to a Funding Code, of which Pt 1, s 11 deals with family and children cases. Proceedings under the Children Act 1989 (the 'Children Act') Pts IV and V (now referred to as 'Special Children Act Proceedings') have the same criteria as before, that is, no means and no merits tests for representation for:

(a) children;

(b) parents;

(c) others with parental responsibility for the child.

Application forms are CLSAPP5

Other Children Act cases have different tests, which are set out in detail in Hershman, D and McFarlane, A, *Children Law and Practice*, Bristol:

Figure 10: Table of enforcement procedures for Children Act orders

Breach of Order	Injunction/ Penal Notice	Surety Bond	Committal or Contempt	Other remedy available	Police Powers and Criminal Proceedings
Refusal to give up a child for Residence Order			RSC Ord 45 r 7 CCR Ord 29 r 1 High Court or county court may commit Family Proc Court may use s 63(3) MCA 1980	Search and Recovery Order s 34 Family Law Reform Act 1986	
Threat to remove child from UK, or actual removal attempt		can be used to ensure return of child	as above	'Seek & Find' High Court Inherent jurisdiction 1) Port Alert System 2) Passport Restriction	1) Police duty to assist where threat of danger or breach of the peace 2) Child Abduction & Custody Act 1985 offence
Change of name when child subject to residence order, w/o consent or leave	✔		✔		
Refusal to comply with s 8 Contact Order	To use penal notice the acts to be enforced must be set out clearly in the order		Committal is rare, but possible	s 34 Family Law Reform Act 1986 possible, combined with s 11(7) directions	
Breach of specific issue or prohibited steps	✔		✔		Police duty to assist where threat of danger may be used in medical emergency

BREACH OF ORDER	INJUNCTION/ PENAL NOTICE	SURETY BOND	COMMITTAL OR CONTEMPT	OTHER REMEDY AVAILABLE	POLICE POWERS AND CRIMINAL PROCEEDINGS
Removal of child from care (under s 31 order)	If removal from jurisdiction is threatened		✔	Port alert if threat to remove from UK High Court Tipstaff if threat to remove from jurisdiction Recovery order s 50 Children Act 1989	Child Abduction & Custody Act 1985 offence Police duty to assist where threat of danger may be used in medical emergency
Chance of name of child in s 31 care without leave/ consent	✔		✔		
Failure to produce records to guardian *ad litem* in care/supervision proceedings	Application to produce documents under s 42 Children Act 1989		Application to court to produce documents under s 42 Children Act 1989		
Breach of directions of the court in Children Act 1989 proceedings, as to filing, service or attendance				• Wasted Costs Order • Court may impose adjourn-ment, or proceed in absence of party • Evidence may be disallowed – but rare in Children Act cases	

Family Law, Pt L, s 3). The main difference is in private law cases (for example, contact and residence applications) where there is a requirement for consideration of mediated solutions before the matter is taken to court. Representation will be refused if there is not more than a 50% chance of success and unless the likely benefits to be gained from the proceedings for the client justify the likely cost. How these nebulous issues are precisely adjudicated is unclear, and even less clear is how the 'benefits' to an adult applicant for, say, contact, should be evaluated where a child's welfare is concerned.

Application forms CLSAPP3 with means forms CLSMEANS1–2 and form L17 required for all applicants including children

For all other applications (for example, judicial review), use forms CLSAPP1, with CLSMEANS 1–2 and Form L17 required for all applicants including children; and for emergency applications, CLSAPP6/6a.

17.2   Appeals and judicial review

Appeals are discussed briefly in these practice notes under each topic, but since there is limited space, judicial review, complaints procedures and appeals procedures can only be mentioned, giving further references. Hershman and McFarlane have an excellent section on judicial review and appeals in Vol 1, s I. Other useful books are: Manning, J, *Judicial Review Proceedings*, 1995, London: Legal Action Group; Fordham, M, *Judicial Review Handbook*, 1994, Chichester: Wiley; and Paynter, ER, *Applicant's Guide to Judicial Review*, 1995, London: Sweet & Maxwell.

17.2.1   Family proceedings court appeals to the High Court

There is no 'slip rule', and no power to review or re-hear a decision. What is pronounced by the chair of the Bench must be written up as the order, and amendment can only happen if the words are not accurately written down. Orders are challenged by notice of appeal within seven days of interim care or supervision orders, or 14 days otherwise, or by way of case stated to the High Court under s 94(1) of the Children Act, Ord 55, r 1(1)(2) Rules of the Supreme Court and r 4.22 Family Proceedings Rules 1991 SI 1991/1247.

17.2.2   County court appeals

Appeal lies from decisions of the district judge to a judge of the same court, r 4.22(4) Family Proceedings Rules 1991.

The county court has the power to review interim, *ex parte* or interlocutory orders; or to rehear its own decisions where there has been no error of the court. In other cases there may be an application to discharge the order, or the parties may serve notice of appeal within 14 days of the decision to the Court of Appeal and are governed by RSC Ord 59.

17.2.3   High Court appeals

Appeal lies from decisions of a district judge to a judge of the same court, for rehearing, no leave required, RSC Ord 58 r 1.

The High Court has the power to review interim, *ex parte* or interlocutory orders; or to rehear its own decisions where there has been no error of the court, s 17 of the Supreme Court Act. In other cases there may be an application to discharge the order, or the parties may serve notice of appeal within 14 days of the decision to the Court of Appeal. Procedure is governed by Ord 59 Rules of the Supreme Court.

Occasionally, appeals may 'leapfrog' by certificate granted under s 12(1) of the Administration of Justice Act 1969 direct to the House of Lords.

17.3 Complaints procedures

If any person wishes to complain about any action by the Department of Social Services in relation to a child, the procedure is set out in the Representations Procedure (Children) Regulations 1991 SI 1991/ 894. The policies which underpin the rights of 'service users', and the way in which complaints should be handled, are set out in: Vols 1–9 of *The Children Act 1989 Guidance and Regulations*; *The Care of Children, Principles and Practice in Regulations and Guidance*, 1991, London: HMSO; and Department of Health and Social Services Inspectorate, *The Right to Complain*, 1991, London: HMSO.

17.4 Enforcement

Enforcement of orders made under the Children Act is discussed briefly in these practice notes under each topic. Further detail is available from Hershman and McFarlane's *Children Law and Practice,* which has an excellent section on enforcement of Children Act orders in Vol 1, part C, s 8, and their table of enforcement procedures for Children Act orders, pp 335–41.

18 Expert Evidence

18.1 Instructing experts

An expert witness is one who is accepted by the court as an expert in a specialist field.

In the course of proceedings in the High Court, Wall J has given helpful guidance in his judgments on the use of expert witnesses and in two cases in particular – *Re M (Minors) (Care Proceedings: Childrens' Wishes)* [1994] 1 FLR 749 and *Re G (Minors) (Expert Witnesses)* [1994] 2 FLR 291, but last year he has brought out a new book with Iain Hamilton, *A Handbook for Expert Witnesses in Children Act Cases,* 2000, Bristol: Family Law. Written for witnesses, but good reading for lawyers, they set out in detail the way in which experts can expect to be approached, issues concerning disclosure, the preparation of instructions and reports. The rules relating to expert evidence in Children Act 1989 (the 'Children Act') cases are the Family Proceedings Courts (Children Act) Rules 1989, r 18 and the Family Proceedings Rules 1989, r 4.18; the Rules of the Supreme Court, Ord 38, rr 35–44; and the County Court Rules, Ord 20, rr 27–28. Pt 35 of the Civil Procedure Rules 1998 also now applies to ancillary relief applications in Children Act cases.

See also the *Handbook of Best Practice in Children Act Cases*, Children Act Advisory Committee, 1997, London: HMSO, and the *Expert Witness Pack for Use in Children Act Proceedings*, Expert Witness Group, 1997, Bristol: Family Law.

Expert instruction checklist

Leave and appropriate consents

(a)   Obtain all necessary leave for instruction of expert and for examination of a child (see Family Proceedings Courts (Children Act) Rules 1989, r 18 and Family Proceedings Rules 1989, r 4.18.

(b)   Obtain leave for disclosure of necessary documents to the expert (see Family Proceedings Courts (Children Act) Rules 1989, r 23 and Family Proceedings Rules 1989, r 4.23).

(c)   Obtain consents from child and those with parental responsibility for examinations and assessments where appropriate (see Chapters 3 and 12 above).

(d)   Discuss instruction of expert with other parties, try to agree joint experts wherever possible.

Note that leave should be given preferably for a named expert, or at least the area of expertise; the issues to be addressed; the date by which the letter of instruction should be sent; documents to be released; and a date for filing the report. Examinations of a child may require directions as to venue, timing, who is to accompany the child and to whom the results should be given.

Letters of instruction should:

(a)   set out the context in which expert opinion sought;

(b)   be accompanied by a chronology and background information;

(c)   provide the expert with all relevant information;

(d)   request the expert to ask for further information or documentation if necessary;

(e)   define specific questions expert is to address;

(f)   contain a request to discuss with other experts and prepare a joint statement or letter defining those issues of agreement and those in dispute;

(g)   be filed at court with list of accompanying documents, and served on other parties;

(h)   if possible, be agreed with other parties but this is not compulsory, see *Re CB and JB (Care Proceedings: Guidelines)* [1998] 2 FLR 211.

Reports, expert conferences, updating, agreed evidence and points in issue

(a) Invite experts to confer together, identifying areas of agreement and disputed issues.

(b) Encourage co-operation between parties and experts.

(c) Co-operate on timing of conferences, reports and evidence.

(d) Ensure that experts are kept up to date with developments in the case relevant to their opinion.

(e) Objectivity – experts should not be biased in any way.

(f) Do not attempt to influence or 'edit' expert reports.

(g) Reports must be disclosed to all parties and the court.

18.2 Expert evidence in court

With careful planning by advocates, the time and patience of expert witnesses can be saved considerably. Joint consultations and jointly compiled experts' lists of agreed and disputed issues save time, whilst arrangement of evidence in a logical sequence to fit the needs of witnesses and the run of the evidence is vital. Agreed written evidence can be admitted by agreement, and witnesses' time saved by attendance for cross examination.

18.3 Finances for expert evidence

Private funding is a matter of negotiation between client, solicitor and expert.

In *publicly funded cases*, the Legal Services Commission now issues Legal Representation certificates, and there are limitations on funding. High cost cases (over £25,000) are dealt with by the Special Cases Unit and the lawyer needs to have an overall cost case plan.

Careful negotiation of expert fees is required in advance of the case to obtain prior authority for instruction of the expert.

Additional unforseen expense in respect of the expert's assessment or report preparation arising after the initial authority must be addressed by an increase in the cost limitation that has been agreed with the Legal Services Commission for the case.

In county court or High Court cases, the detailed assessment (new form of taxation) may mean a reduction in the fees allowed for expert evidence, and the expert needs to be made aware of this possibility.

Payments may be made on account of work completed by experts, within a month of invoice and claim, but frequently the Legal Services Commission allows up to 75% of the full amount where there may be a detailed assessment and consequent reduction of fees allowed.

18.4   Finding the right expert

The most effective way of finding experts is recommendation by other legal practitioners in similar work. Ask expert(s) to disclose qualifications, current work and relevant past experience – not only for reassurance, but also because to do so is useful for the court, other parties and the legal aid board. Ask how often the expert has given evidence in court before – they may be brilliant on paper, but terrible at giving oral evidence.

The list of registers and directories below may be a starting point in the search for the right expert.

18.4.1   Experts lists, registers and directories

Some of these organisations will send out published lists. Others provide information in response to a telephone or written enquiry, and may charge an administration fee.

Organisation	Title
British Psychological Society	*Directory of Chartered Psychologists*
The Forensic Science Society	*World List of Forensic Science Laboratories and Practices*
The Forensic Science Society	*Register of Independent Consultants*
JS Publications	*UK Register of Expert Witnesses*
Law Society	*Expert Witness Register*
British Academy of Experts	*Register of Experts*

Journals and supplements

Expert Evidence (International Digest of Human Behaviour, Science and Law)	SLE Publications
Solicitors Journal	Expert Witnesses Supplement
Law Society Gazette	Expert Witness Supplement

Lawyers' lists

Law Society's Children Panel	Membership List
London Criminal Courts Solicitors Association	Agency and Membership List
Association of Lawyers for Children	Experts database

Useful information on instructing experts

A Handbook for Expert Witnesses in Children Act Cases	Mr Justice Wall with Iain Hamilton, 2000, Bristol: Family Law
Expert Witness Pack for Use in Children Act Proceedings	1997, Expert Witness Group: Family Law
Handbook of Best Practice in Children Act Cases	1997, Children Act Advisory Committee, London: HMSO/DoH
Expert Evidence Law and Practice	Hodgkinson, T, 1990, London: Sweet & Maxwell
Forensic Medicine for Lawyers	Mason, JK, 1990, London: Butterworths
Medical Law: Text with Materials	Kennedy, I and Grubb, A, 2nd edn, 1994, London: Butterworths

19 Information, Guidance and Reference Works

19.1 Child protection essential information library

The Children Act 1989 Guidance and Regulations (1991, London: HMSO) comprising:

Volume 1	Court Orders	ISBN 0 11321 371 9
Volume 2	Family Support, Day Care and Educational Provision for Young Children	ISBN 0 11321 372 7
Volume 3	Family Placements	ISBN 0 11321 375 1
Volume 4	Residential Care	ISBN 0 11321 430 8
Volume 5	Independent Schools	ISBN 0 11321 373 5
Volume 6	Children with Disabilities	ISBN 0 11321 452 9
Volume 7	Guardians ad Litem and Other Court Related Issues	ISBN 0 11321 471 5
Volume 8	Private Fostering and Miscellaneous	ISBN 0 11321 473 1
Volume 9	Adoption Issues I	ISBN 0 11321 474 X
Volume 10	Index	ISBN 0 11321 538 X

Working Together to Safeguard Children, London: HMSO

Assessing Children in Need and their Families, 2000, London: HMSO

Framework for Assessment of Children in Need and their Families, 2000, London: HMSO

Area Child Protection Committee Manual (local copy obtainable from the ACPC Chair)

Children Act Advisory Committee Directions, Pro Formas, Public and Private Law, London: CAAC

A child and family law reference work, regularly updated (see 19.2 below)

The Report of the Inquiry into Child Abuse in Cleveland, 1987, London: HMSO

The Care of Children, Principles and Practice in Regulations and Guidance, 1991, London: HMSO

A book on child development (see below)

Sample set of *Sheffield Centile Charts* with accompanying notes (obtainable from a GP or Health Visitor)

UN Convention on the Rights of the Child 1992

European Convention for the Protection of Human Rights and Fundamental Freedoms 1950

Protocols made under the European Convention for the Protection of Human Rights and Fundamental Freedoms 1950

List(s) of expert witnesses

Family/child law reports

Family/child law journals/newsletters

Memorandum of Good Practice in Video Recorded Interviews of Children, 1992, London: HMSO

Interviewing Child Witnesses under the Memorandum of Good Practice, 1999, London: Home Office

19.2 Reading and reference list

Practice guidance

Handbook of Best Practice in Children Act Cases, Children Act Advisory Committee, 1997, London: HMSO

Guidance for Solicitors Acting for Children in Private Law Proceedings under the Children Act 1989, 1994, Solicitors Family Law Committee

Guidance for Solicitors Working with Guardians ad Litem, 1986, The Law Society's Family Law Committee, and subsequently revised, London: The Law Society

Guide to Good Practice for Solicitors Acting for Children, 2000, Solicitors Family Law Association, available from SFLA, PO Box 302 Orpington, Kent BR6 8QX (£5 to non-members)

Looseleaf reference works

Bromley, PM (ed), *The Family Law Service,* London: Butterworths (3 volumes)

Hershman, D and McFarlane, A (eds), *Children Law and Practice,* 1991, Bristol: Family Law

Hoggett, B (ed), *Clarke Hall and Morrison on Children,* London: Butterworths

Jones, RM (ed), *The Encyclopaedia of Social Services and Child Care Law,* London: Sweet & Maxwell

Child law books

Adcock, M, White, R and Hollows, A (eds), *Significant Harm,* 1991, Croydon: Significant

King, P and Young, I, *The Child as Client,* 1992, Bristol: Family Law

Levy, A (ed) *Re-focus on Child Abuse,* 1994, London: Hawkesmere

Liddle, C, *Acting for Children,* 1992, London: The Law Society

Monro, P and Forrester, L, *The Guardian ad Litem,* 1995, Bristol: Family Law

Timms, JE, *Children's Representation, A Practitioner's Guide,* London: Sweet & Maxwell

Forensic investigation of child abuse

Dent, H and Flin, R (eds), *Children as Witnesses*, 1996, Chichester: Wiley

Meadow, R, *ABC of Child Abuse*, 1997, London: BMA

Reder, P, Duncan, S and Gray, M, *Beyond Blame*, 1993, London: Routledge

Memorandum of Good Practice in Interviewing Child Witnesses, 1991, London: HMSO

Child development

Holt, KS, *Child Development – Diagnosis and Assessment*, 1994, London: Butterworth Heinemann

Useful information

Brennan, C, *The Directory of Child Rights and Welfare*, 1990, Cambridge: Woodhead-Faulken

Department of Health and Social Services Inspectorate, *The Right to Complain*, 1991, London: HMSO

Expert Witness Group, *Expert Witness Pack for Use in Children Act Proceedings*, 1997, Bristol: Family Law

Friel, J, *Children with Special Needs*, 4th edn, 1997, London: Jessica Kingsley

Thorpe LJ (Rt Hon) and Clarke, E, *Divided Duties*, 1998, Bristol: Family Law

Valman, HB, *ABC of One to Seven*, 1993, London: BMJ

Wall LJ (Rt Hon) (ed), *Rooted Sorrows*, 1997, Bristol: Family Law

Wall J (Hon) with Hamilton, I, *A Handbook for Expert Witnesses in Children Act Cases*, 2000, Bristol: Family Law

National Standards for Probation Service Family Court Welfare Work, London: Home Office

Computer software

Family Law, a new Justis CD ROM, full text of Family Law reports since 1980, searchable by name, topic, etc

Children Law and Practice and *Family Law Reports*, Family Law CD ROM, available from The Stationery Office Limited (formerly HMSO) Publications Centre:

Telephone orders	0870 600 5522
Website	www.hmso.gov.uk
Online bookstore	www.clicktso.com

Specialist law updates

Practitioners Guide to Child Law	Remy Zentar (ed), available from: 24 Rathen Road Withington Manchester M20 9GH
Family Law Reports	Jordans, Family Law
Family Court Reports	Jordans, Family Law
Practitioners Child Law Bulletin	Longman
Journal of Child Law	Tolley
Family Law Directory	Jordans, Family Law

Training

Family Law, Central Law Training and other Law Society accredited training organisations offer Child and Family Law Training.

Family Law training:	www.jordanpublishing.co.uk/ seminars.html
The Law Society website :	www.lawsociety.org.uk
Central Law Training website:	www.centlaw.com

For Children Panel training, see below, Chapter 20.

20 Improving Law, Skills and Practice

It is necessary for lawyers to keep up to date with statute and case law and to constantly develop knowledge and skills, not only in law but, for example, in medicine, psychology and parenting. It is vital to maintain a list of resources to which child clients and families may be referred and it helps to belong to organisations which can provide information and assistance. In those areas of the country where child law practitioners may find themselves isolated, discussion with a network of colleagues provides moral and practical support.

20.1 Interdisciplinary associations

Association of Lawyers for Children

The Administrator
PO Box 2029
Buckhurst Hill
Essex IG9 6EQ

www.alc.org.uk
admin@alc.org.uk

British Association for Adoption
and Fostering

Secretary
Skyline House
200 Union Street,
London SE1 0LX

Tel: 020 7593 2000
Fax: 020 7593 2001

www.baaf.org.uk
mail@baaf.org.uk

British Association for the Study
and Prevention of Child Abuse

and Neglect (BASPCAN)

National Administrator
10 Priory Street
York YO1 1EZ

Tel: 01904 613605
Fax: 01904 642239

www.baspcan@baspcan.org.uk
mail@baspcan.org.uk

National Youth Advisory Service

1 Downham Road South
Heswall
Wirral
Merseyside CH60 5RG

Tel: 0151 342 7852
Fax: 0151 342 3174

www.nyas.net
nyas@charity.vfree.com

Solicitors Family Law Association

Secretary
Mary L'Anson
PO Box 302
Orpington
Kent BR6 8QX

Tel: 01689 850227
Fax: 01689 855833

www.sfla.co.uk
sfla@btinternet.com

Local Guardian ad Litem and
Solicitor Groups

Check with local
Guardian Panel Managers

NAGALRO (National Association
for Guardians ad Litem and
Reporting Officers)

c/o National Children's
Bureau
8 Wakely Street
London EC1V 7QE

Tel: 020 7843 6008

www.nagalro.com

20.2 The Law Society's Children Panel

The Children Panel comprises practitioners specialising in representation of children, families and local authorities in public or private law matters. For membership, applicants must have post-qualification experience in child and family law and a sound knowledge of child law and practice. In addition, they need an understanding of child development and of child related issues, for example, contact and care planning. They also undergo specific training to develop their skills in communicating with children.

Children Panel membership is a recognition of this specialist training and experience, and therefore constitutes one of the criteria for claiming enhanced remuneration in Children Act cases.

Solicitors wishing to be accepted for membership of the Children Panel must produce evidence of the appropriate qualifications and relevant experience; acquire the necessary training; and, on application, will be asked to submit written answers to questions from the Law Society. Finally, they must pass a selection interview.

Children Panel training courses are comprehensive, covering a wide range of law and topics relevant to the representation of children, families and local authorities and working with the guardian ad litem.

Information about the Children Panel, lists of training courses, and application forms can be obtained from Christine Caswell at The Law Society, Ipsley Court, Redditch, Worcestershire B98 0TD.